# WARNING SIGNS OF ABUSE

# WARNING SIGNS OF ABUSE
## GET OUT EARLY AND STAY FREE FOREVER

## THERESA WERBA

BARDSINGER BOOKS

## Books by Theresa Werba

*What Was and Is: Formal Poetry and Free Verse*
*Sonnets*
*Longer Thoughts*
*Jesus and Eros: Sonnets, Poems, and Songs*
*Warning Signs of Abuse: Get Out Early and Stay Free Forever*
*When Adoption Fails: Abuse, Autism, and the Search for My Identity*
*Diaper Changes: The Complete Diapering Book and Resource Guide*

Upcoming:
*Finally Autistic: Finding My Autism Diagnosis as a Middle-Aged Female*

ISBN: 978-0-965955-1-0
KINDLE EDITION AISN # B00TU4DUZO
http://www.bardsinger.com BARDSINGER BOOKS
Copyright ©2015 THERESA WERBA
Cover design by: Francesca Farrisi (www.francescafarrisi.com)

*To Nicole Brown Simpson (May 19, 1959 - June 12, 1994)*

# TABLE OF CONTENTS

READ THIS FIRST: WARNING ABOUT WARNING SIGNS OF
ABUSE                                                                    - 11 -

PREFACE                                                                  - 13 -

CHAPTER ONE: THE WEB OF ABUSE                                           - 15 -
   *THE CYCLE OF ABUSE*                                   - 16 -
   *YOU BELONG TO ME*                                     - 17 -

CHAPTER TWO: PROFILE OF THE ABUSER                                      - 19 -
   *THE NARCISSIST*                                       - 19 -
   *THE SOCIOPATH AND THE PSYCHOPATH*                     - 21 -
   *THE LITTLE BOY*                                       - 23 -
   *POWER AND CONTROL*                                    - 24 -
   *A BULLY AND A COWARD ARE THE SAME THING*              - 24 -

CHAPTER THREE: PROFILE OF THE TARGET WOMAN                              - 27 -
   *HEY THERE, LONELY GIRL*                               - 27 -
   *NAIVETE AND EXPERIENCE*                               - 28 -
   *CHILDHOOD AND PREVIOUS ABUSE*                         - 29 -
   *LOOKING FOR LOVE IN ALL THE WRONG PLACES*             - 30 -
   *SMART WOMEN, FOOLISH CHOICES*                         - 31 -

CHAPTER FOUR: PHASES IN THE ABUSE PROCESS: FROM NICE
TO NO WAY OUT                                                            - 35 -
   *PHASE ONE: SO BEGUILING*                              - 35 -

*PHASE TWO: MOST CRITICAL: A PEEK INTO HIS PAST AND YOUR FUTURE* - 37 -

*PHASE THREE: THE ABUSE BEGINS; THE WEB GETS STICKY* - 41 -

*PHASE FOUR: GETTING WORSE AND NEW WAYS OF COPING* - 47 -

*PHASE FIVE: CRISIS PROPORTIONS AND NEW LIFE SKILLS* - 52 -

*PHASE SIX: COUNSELING* - 53 -

*PHASE SEVEN: THE LAW* - 54 -

*PHASE EIGHT: ATTEMPTING TO GET OUT* - 56 -

*PHASE NINE: THE CYCLE OR YOUR FREEDOM?* - 57 -

**CHAPTER FIVE: WHAT TO DO WHEN YOU CANNOT GET OUT** - 61 -

*TO THOSE ON THE OUTSIDE LOOKING IN* - 61 -

*WHY ARE YOU STILL THERE?* - 63 -

*COPING AND MAINTAINING* - 79 -

*KEEPING RECORDS* - 83 -

*COUNSELING AND SUPPORT* - 85 -

**CHAPTER SIX: NICOLE BROWN SIMPSON (1959-1994) AND OJ SIMPSON** - 87 -

*THE VOICE OF NICOLE BROWN SIMPSON* - 89 -

*WHAT HAPPENED IN THE LIFE OF NICOLE BROWN SIMPSON, AND WHY WAS SHE MURDERED BY OJ SIMPSON?* - 92 -

*THE AFTERMATH AND LEGACY OF THE OJ SIMPSON VERDICT* - 97 -

**CHAPTER SEVEN: CONTROL YOURSELF: A PARADIGM SHIFT IN THE TREATMENT OF ABUSERS** - 101 -

*AGAINST POSITIVE AFFIRMATION* - 101 -

*NOT AVOIDING PAIN AND SUFFERING*                    - 101 -

*CONTROL YOURSELF, NOT OTHERS*                    - 102 -

**CHAPTER EIGHT: I CLIMBED UP AND AWAY— AND YOU CAN, TOO**                                                          - 105 -

*SEVEN TIME'S THE CHARM*                              - 105 -

*WHY DO WE GO BACK?*                                 - 105 -

*KEYS TO BREAKING FREE*                              - 109 -

*THE FEARS AND REALITIES OF A PROTECTIVE ORDER*   - 113 -

*WHY PROTECTIVE ORDERS DON'T ALWAYS WORK*        - 124 -

*OTHER LEGAL ISSUES: SEPARATION, DIVORCE, CUSTODY, CHILD SUPPORT, AND TAXES*                              - 126 -

*STARTING OVER*                                      - 131 -

**EPILOGUE: A FUTURE FREE FROM ABUSE**            - 135 -

**ADDENDUM: ABUSE SEX**                              - 139 -

**ACKNOWLEDGMENTS**                                  - 147 -

**SOURCES AND RESOURCES**                            - 149 -

**ABOUT THE AUTHOR**                                 - 151 -

# READ THIS FIRST: WARNING ABOUT WARNING SIGNS OF ABUSE

Do not read *Warning Signs of Abuse* in your home, unless you can be very sure your abuser cannot catch you reading it or find it on your Kindle, iPad, computer or phone. Read it somewhere private and safe, such as a friend's house, home of a family member, or if you can be secure at work or school or at a public library. If you are reading a Kindle e-book, you want to be able to close it and/or log off quickly if necessary. This will work if he does not have access to your online accounts. Only tell people you trust that you are reading it, people that will not tell your abuser about it. Do not ever read it when he is present. Do not ever tell him you are reading it. Do not mention its name to him. Do not taunt him or incite him in any way about it. Use this book as a tool to get free from your abusive situation. But do not let it become a means through which he can abuse you even more.

# PREFACE

I have written this book to help women get out of abusive relationships. You may have just met him or have been with him or married for years. I am also writing with particular attention to the "warning signs" or "red flags" in abusive relationships— words and situations and actions and behaviors that should be indicators that the relationship is becoming abusive or is going to become abusive. I am writing to help women get out of abusive relationships as early as possible and stay out of them forever.

I spent twenty-one years in an abusive marriage, two additional years with him before I married him, and two years living with him after we were legally divorced. I write from a wealth of experience and hindsight and research and reflection. I have struggled with every aspect of the entanglement of abuse, but even though it took me a long time I really did do it and I really am finally free. This is the future I want any women to have who is in an abusive relationship, and I want her to have it sooner that I had it.

I am writing so that you can see the warning signs when the relationship in just starting out, so you can get away before it entangles you. I am also writing to those ensnared to give directions and hope for getting out. Although there are many kinds of abusive relationships, I am writing to females who are victims of abuse from males. This is the paradigm under which I choose to be specific. I am not addressing issues of incest or child abuse or homosexual abuse. I am confident, however, that anyone caught in abuse can find useful information in this book and might make application of it to situations other than the one about which I am directing my attention. It is my earnest hope and expectation that many women in abuse will find the information, tools and encouragement needed to get out early and stay free forever. —Theresa Werba

# CHAPTER ONE: THE WEB OF ABUSE

It is that spark of vulnerability, that something that allows for the connection to happen, the meeting of the emotional stars. It may seem so satisfying and curious at first but it is more than anything you may have had before and maybe in some ways it is better. The intensity of it, the rush, the speed, the love-talk, the love act, doesn't it all happen so fast?

Within the speed is the dangerous whirl, that spinning vortex that before you can climb out of it you have begun to be sucked into it. It happens when you are so caught in the moment of the thrill and the chase that you do not see that the vortex is turning and you are yourself turning and turning. But what was it that drew you in? That spot, that place of vulnerability, that area in the heart that likes being flattered and charmed and made to feel that beautiful and important or valuable.

And before the vortex is done swirling you and around and whirling you into a powder, other things are entering in. The intensity of the vortex begins to have dark chakras, the energy goes sideways, the shock value begins to shock. *Am I different now that he is in my life? Did I do something wrong here? Is he just in a bad mood? Why do I get this feeling of foreboding? Why does this weird sense of fear come upon me?* Of course it is just that this is so new and real and intense and wonderful, but why do I feel afraid somehow and why does part of me want to get away?

That vortex entraps because of the speed at which it develops and the less powerful nature of the object that gets caught within the whirl and swirl. The speed is a device, and it can be a tool in the arsenal of the dominator seeking prey to dominate. Beware, oh deer in the headlights, for those pretty lights aiming into your eyes is the vortex coming to suck you in as you stare back unawares!

## THE CYCLE OF ABUSE

And so it starts this way. Within that whirl and swirl is some kind of pain, some kind of shock. You feel the nausea combined with dread. Maybe I can't go on these kinds of rides, maybe I am not cut out for them, maybe I should try something else, or sit this out a while. For a moment it slows and the nice energy returns and the nice strokes and pats return and the daisies in the field are under your feet again and the blues and whites of the princess and her long hair are dancing before your vision eyes again. *Perhaps I will get used to the speed of it, after all I just need some practice, perhaps maybe I caused the vortex to swing so hard around. I will go into the purple colors and swirl again.* Purple is the color of rich blood vessels when they are broken, but so pretty a color it is indeed, is it not?

The vortex is a wheel, not the up and around of a Ferris wheel, but a sucking circling kind of wheel that spins and ignites from the energy that is in it, and that energy is you. Without you, the vortex would seek another energy, and with you, it becomes more alive and it swirls faster, and you feel the swirl and it is fast and exciting and a bit nauseating and a bit scary. In some ways it is better than the damp green grass of ordinary and fields of buttercups and daisies. And then the vortex shocks you once more, a little more of your energy is taken from you, you feel the depletion and yet you seem to stay. *But then should I get off? Can I get out?* But by the time you think again about it, the vortex has begun to embed itself into your legs and body, and you are embedded into it as well, those colors of purple and yellow and red, fire and bruised blood! And as you try to rid yourself of this vortex ride, behold! the sweet "sorries" come again, you hear the melodious strains of remorse, which sound as real as all the lute songs and trumpets in fairy land. *What is outside this spinning anyway? Maybe I can get adjusted to this, after all, being sorry is so nice, since it keeps the spinning going round and around!*

But mark me, the purples will come again against the fiery reds and yellows, the colors of anger and heat and the conversion of your energy into the vortex, and those purples will even crack open to show the red from which they are truly made. Again and again and again and again and again.

## YOU BELONG TO ME

The man in the middle of the vortex is the vortex itself, who both creates it and sustains himself by keeping you in it. Without you, the force would starve and grow angry. Then the force will cajole you back to itself with charms and potions that appeal to the heart. The thing that has grown from the two of you together is greater than the sum of your two parts. And without you upon which to feed and glean, the vortex will rise in greater fury to encapsulate you so that you cannot wrench your shoulder to be free or move your legs to run away. The fairy land was in the vortex was it not, or was it? That dragon was not me, or him, was it? You then belong to it. Do you accept this new identity? Do you think if you remain in the vortex that all will be the goodness and nice energies again? Do you?

I know all these feelings and realities because I experienced them all. The whirlwind beginning, the emotional state of vulnerability I was in at the time, the intensity of the movement of the relationship so early on, getting into a ride that was going so fast I did not realize how far I was getting from the old world of normal until I was so enmeshed in it I found it hard to get away. My mind had already been altered to think differently, my ears had been acclimated to hearing cursing and put-downs, and eventually when the purple bruises came, I somehow thought I deserved them and that I made them happen somehow. And then when the red roses of repentance came in a bundle I would relent and return again. Eventually I returned even when there were no roses or even any "sorries" said to me any more at all.

Abuse causes a change in the psyche and in the biochemistry of a woman. It can on the one hand bring in the "fight or flight" response which heightens your sense of tension and fear. It can alternately be expressed in "behavioral inaction," where the shock of the situation literally freezes you into staying still. Sometimes it makes you unable to think and then you feel numbed. Then when some part of sense returns and you see the danger in the fight or flight response, the repentant acts or words of your abuser draw you back in again. And there is a calming after that storm, like the afterglow of orgasm. This will remain until the next tension develops (as in your trying to pull away) or the grip tightens because the appetite of the abuser for control over you has increased. But as the day rises and as the moon cycles through her phases, the cycle of abuse will continue and worsen unless you can get away and stay away. I am hoping to show you that is can be done, and the earlier the better, if you see the warning signs of abuse for what they are and move swiftly and resolutely away early so you can stay free forever.

# CHAPTER TWO: PROFILE OF THE ABUSER

## THE NARCISSIST

Narcissus was the Greek god who loved his own reflection in the water so much that trying to kiss himself he fell in the lake and drowned. It is a metaphor for the type of error that can cause a person to love himself or think so highly of himself that he causes his own destruction.

I think abusers are narcissistic because they have a great and perverted sense of self-importance. This combines a bit with misogynistic attitudes of feeling superior to women and even having some kind of hatred or contempt for women— however they might like them sexually or for how they may help them have children or keep their home clean. I think they resent that women have any identity or importance apart from their place in their world, which is the only world that exists to the narcissist. This is why they are incredulous when you want to leave and angry that you have any desire or ability to assert yourself in efforts to get away from the pain and hurt he is causing you. It reminds me of that satirical old Hank Williams song, "Put Another Log On The Fire," which combines the best of narcissism and misogyny:

> "*Put another log on the fire.*
> *Cook me up some bacon and some beans.*
> *And go out to the car and change the tire.*
> *Wash my socks and sew my old blue jeans.*
> *Come on, baby, you can fill my pipe,*
> *And then go fetch my slippers.*
> *And boil me up another pot of tea.*

*Then put another log on the fire, babe,*
*And come and tell me why you're leaving me.*

*Now don't I let you wash the car on Sunday?*
*Don't I warn you when you're gettin fat?*
*Ain't I a-gonna take you fishin' with me someday?*
*Well, a man can't love a woman more than that.*
*Ain't I always nice to your kid sister?*
*Don't I take her driving every night?*
*So, sit here at my feet 'cos I like you when you're sweet,*
*And you know it ain't feminine to fight.*

*So, put another log on the fire.*
*Cook me up some bacon and some beans.*
*Go out to the car and lift it up and change the tire.*
*Wash my socks and sew my old blue jeans.*
*Come on, baby, you can fill my pipe,*
*And then go fetch my slippers.*
*And boil me up another pot of tea.*
*Then put another log on the fire, babe,*
*And come and tell me why you're leaving me. "*

©Sheldon Silverstein 1974

The narcissist is incapable of believing he is not the object of the world's affection and attention and is most offended when someone give him a de facto "rejection" by attempting to pull away from a relationship— even more so when it is abusive. They do not see themselves as abusive, but benign, even benevolent, and certainly justified in their anger towards you— who causes their feelings to be disturbed, who fails to recognize their worth, who neglects to respect and appreciate them. It is never, ever a case where they failed to respect and treat you with dignity, to honor you, to value your worth, or find you in equal value to himself. The curse of the narcissist is his own self-love that blinds him to the pain which he can cause others through his own selfishness.

You will most likely see the narcissist in your abuser when you try to leave or get away. *"What? How dare she! who does she think she is? doesn't she know what she's got? she'll never do better than me! that little ingrate! I am the best thing that has ever happened to her, she'll be sorry if she tries to leave me! the nerve of her! she won't be able to make it without me! I am what makes her world go 'round!"*

## THE SOCIOPATH AND THE PSYCHOPATH

Some psychologists and sociologists say that a sociopath and a psychopath are interchangeable terms, but I have seen those who say they mean related but different things. I think there are sociopaths and I think there are psychopaths. "Path" refers to "pathology" or the study of illness or disease (literally, the "suffering"); I like the gradation of pathology the two terms are afforded if one thinks of a sociopath as having more of an issue of illness with how he relates socially, whereas a psychopath refers more to a person with a severe disease of the psyche or soul. Sociopaths tend to be criminals, bullies, drug addicts, even gamblers, even abusers. But a psychopath you should really fear, because they lack the ability to feel human emotion and empathy as do "normal" people. It seems that psychopaths truly do have different brains. Studies are showing a defect in the amygdala of the brain which is a center for feelings and emotion. Researchers have shown violent and disturbing images to normal people and their amygdalae light up with all kinds of CAT scan activity; show those same images to a psychopath and the amygdala is dark. It is a matter of the effect of being evil or is it the cause of being evil? Psychopaths are the cause of horror and terror and suffering to so many— these are the serial killers, the ones who kill and eat their victims, who rape and kill and bury little boys under their houses, who keep girls tied up for years in the basements, who kill because they like it and hurt because they do not care.

Abusers can be sociopaths and possibly psychopaths. It has been said that not all criminals are psychopaths and not all psychopaths are criminals, so it gets very murky when it comes to abusive relationships. A true psychopath who cannot feel normal empathy for others may be a very successful businessman or lawyer or politician. He has learned the way to act and interact publicly but could be a serial killer, rapist or abuser in an alter-type world where no one sees. It amazes me that these men (and they are predominantly men) can slither through life in the shadow or normalcy but default to a world of the absence of human feeling when they think they can get away with it. They are not sorry that they get arrested, only sorry they get caught. If released they will rape and kill again. The rate of recidivism is extremely high among psychopaths. Some research is looking towards some kind of implant in the brain that could help the amygdala of psychopaths respond like normal humans. Otherwise, one has to wonder if these people are defects or anomalies and if they are truly human in the human sense of the word at all.

It seems that abuse falls into a kind of syndrome of behaviors among the sociopath and psychopath. With sociopaths who are criminals you see drug abuse, gambling, robbery, aggression and assault, gang activity, drinking, fiscal irresponsibility, sort of a cluster of behaviors together, a fragmentation of normal functioning that usually ends the abuser in jail, sometimes because of the abuse applied to his female. Psychopaths seem to be the smarter of the grouping; they can sometimes hurt and kill for years before ever being caught and are clean and neat and thoughtful about how they go about their evils. Sociopaths seem to be "sloppier," perhaps less intelligent, more prone to mistakes and less smart about being caught. Still one has to wonder about any man who hurts a woman or a child— anyone weaker than he is— and can walk around with a happy conscience and justify it. The trouble is the conscience itself. I suppose the truth of the matter is that a psychopath has no conscience and a sociopath has a damaged once. Either way, they can be abusers and they will make your life hell if you get involved with one. And like many women, you can end up injured, emotionally ruined, or dead.

## THE LITTLE BOY

Abusers often act like little boys who hate the their mommy and don't have their daddy to discipline them. They hate the word "no" and they throw tantrums when things are not the way they like it. They are spoiled and temperamental and hyper-sensitive to their own needs and wants. They like being coddled and caressed and pampered and hate it when things do not go their way. Worse of all, they hate it when they cannot control the situation and especially when they cannot control you.

## POWER AND CONTROL

My abuser actually used to say these words to me: "Power and control, it's all about power and control." The problem is that he thought I wanted power and control over him or wanted to take power and control away from him, but all I ever wanted was to be treated the way a woman should be treated and loved in some way and have a happy marriage. The only thing I would have liked to have been able to control was the way he treated me. I never had an interest in controlling his life or having power over him. But he was desperate in his desire to control me and hated it when he could not. And when he could not control me or have power over me, he got the power he craved by reducing me and ridiculing me and making me feel horrible about myself and then getting off on watching me cry or get into an argument. That was the only way he could raise himself up from his own feeling of inadequacy. Reduce me and then climb over the heap that was crying on the floor.

## A BULLY AND A COWARD ARE THE SAME THING

And do you know what I used to say to him? I asked him a simple question, which has a simple answer. *"Do you know what the difference between a bully and a coward is? nothing!"* Because, of course, he was a bully to me, and a coward because he was a bully to me. Nobody is a true man who has to intimidate or assault or hurt someone physically weaker than he is in order to feel good about himself. A weak and insecure man is the coward who hides behind bravado and puffing up the chest and exploding in rage and shouting in intimidation and wielding their stronger arm and hands at you and across you. I have never liked bullies and I have never liked thugs and yet I married a bully and a thug and stayed with him for almost twenty-three years. He bullied me and thugged me and I grew to despise being in his presence. I honestly thought that he had given up the thuggery of his youth when we got together— the fact that he had been a thug at all was a warning sign I should have heeded. How could I have chosen a man who used to beat up homosexuals and taunt old Jewish men? How could I have borne the children of a man who once tied up an old lady so he could steal her jewelry for drug money? There are certain acts and lifestyles which I think forfeit the subsequent procuring of viable human relationships. But I delved into the future that I was seeking, and my own loneliness and desperation to reproduce drove me to the worst possible choice of life companion I could have ever made.

# CHAPTER THREE: PROFILE OF THE TARGET WOMAN

## HEY THERE, LONELY GIRL

Loneliness is one of the saddest states of life and I wish women could learn to be content in being "alone" rather than "lonely." I had many involvements and liaisons at the time I started to get involved with my abuser. I was not really "alone" but lonely in that I wanted to reproduce and the other options were not ripening for me. I had lost the love I thought I had with another man that I was supposed to have married years before, and I was in a state of cynicism and hopelessness that I would ever get married and have a family. I was angry and hurt by the broken promises that were made to me years earlier. I was in that sense lonely, cynical and very, very vulnerable.

But abusers can smell the loneliness and they swoop in to fill the void. They rush with the fastness of the relationship, the words of love so fast, the gifts and the whirlwind and then you so suddenly are not lonely anymore. If anything you are wildly distracted by the energy of it and the vortex, but you do not see that you are entering the vortex and beginning to get swirled within it. Even the depression of loneliness is lifted in the sudden intensity and seeming satisfaction of this remedy and answer.

But beware of who goes after you and the person you go after when you are lonely. That loneliness can turn to desperation and desperation can blind your choices. Even a starving dog will cherish a bone. At first it does not look like a mere bone because the dog has been so hungry. Yes, there may have even been some meat on it but within time he realizes he ate that all so fast and now there is this delicious bone he keeps gnawing and sucking on. But it seems to satisfy and he is not hungry anymore! But truly this animal is still starving, just sucking the bony edges of nothing. Beware of the loneliness that can set out the scent which will trap you!

## NAIVETE AND EXPERIENCE

I have a friend who got sucker-punched into a marriage with a man who was wicked and abusive. They got married a mere six weeks after they met. She was weak and naive and he was the hunter out for the prey. He caught with his greasy charm and fast words and fast actions. He ended up making her mentally ill, terrorizing her life and threatening to harm her parents. He has spent about half of his life in prison for being a chronic and habitual kleptomaniac. He coerced my friend to hold the getaway car while he'd go in stores and shove things into his pants. He reduced an already weak and vulnerable young woman into a fractured and damaged person who bore him two children he never deserved and neither of whom will ever know what it is like to have a proper father.

I have seen many cases of first love being lasting and beautiful. I have friends and family who met as teens and have had good and healthy and happy marriages. But the chance exists that because you are new to love, or are in some way naive and therefore vulnerable, you could become ensnared by an abuser. Often times it is a woman who never had a relationship before. Maybe she has a tenderness of heart that is exploited. Maybe she has a religious or spiritual leaning that is discerned by the abuser and his mental prey-detector— such is the case with so many women who get suckered into cults where the cult leader abuses and takes advantage of multiple women. In the worst of the perverse cults, females are raised and groomed to become sex objects for dirty old men or one of multiple wives of perverts in the name of religion.

And on the other hand, being highly experienced can set you out as prey for the abusive appetite as well. They perceive you as a catch, a challenge to capture. He will want to try to rope you in because so many others had gotten you before him. It may stroke his ego that he managed to ring you in. And even more enticing is the idea of dominating and controlling someone who has been the object of desire to so many before him.

## CHILDHOOD AND PREVIOUS ABUSE

Unfortunately if you were abused as a child you are more likely to end up in an abusive relationship as an adult. I wish this were not true— it seems so doubly unkind to be hurt and wounded as a child by the people who are supposed to love and care for you, only to end up being hurt and wounded again as an adult by the man who is supposed to love you and care for you. But in some ways you get set up for it, a kind of learned response to certain psychic and emotional stimuli. You respond this way now because you responded that way as a child back then. What we learn as children we take with us into adulthood— unless very conscious efforts are made not to repeat patterns learned as a child or fall into an emotionally similar dynamic as an adult. Again, this is the "scent" you give off, a vibe of being vulnerable because you were wounded before. It is like animals in herds or packs, that pick on and sometimes kill (and sometimes eat!) the weakest member of the group.

You must make a conscious effort to realize that you are likely to fall for an abuser if you were abused as a child. You must look long and hard at your choices and be even more circumspect in your choices because of it. Once the abuser starts into you, it will stab like a stingray into your heart and into the recesses of your most primal self. And it will be harder and harder to break away from the thing you grew up believing was normal, no matter how painful or traumatic it was when you were young.

## LOOKING FOR LOVE IN ALL THE WRONG PLACES

It would be helpful to start seeking along a good crop than go picking in the rot of the garbage heap. This is not to say there are no psychopaths among well-bred people, but avoid people involved in vice and you will lessen your chance of finding an abuser. Online dating has worked for many people but I can see it as an insidious way for predator- types to find vulnerable and willing prey. Even worse is the whole subculture of internet mail-order brides, where women desperate to get out of a poor nation will settle for some scum of an American male simply because he has money and holds the promise of American citizenship. I have heard of women who died from the abuse suffered because of marrying one of these vile men.

# SMART WOMEN, FOOLISH CHOICES

I am a smart woman, an educated woman, an intelligent woman, and yet the choice of my life partner lay with a criminal drug user who abused me and nearly destroyed me completely. You can find abusers among kings and among bums. You can be a waitress or a doctor or a princess and you can be abused. It has nothing to do with intelligence or accomplishments or social status or position in society. It has everything to do with getting caught in a web of entanglement that even the smartest woman will find difficult to escape, especially if she does not heed the warning signs early on and get out before it completely entangles her.

Even smart women can become the victims of abuse. Where did I go wrong? I think I was not using my intellect when my gut was telling me something was not right. I have heard it said that the cells in the digestive system are like a "second brain" and that is why we get these premonitions in our stomach or a "feeling" in the guts about something when it is not right. Some people call it premonition. Some call it the "sixth sense." Some people call it "women's intuition." Whatever it is, it is not in your brain cells but in your gut cells or the brain cells in your gut. It is okay to have these sensations or feelings or intuitions because they can alert the actual brain about something it is not sensing otherwise. I think perhaps that this "second brain" is doing what it is supposed to do— giving you that sick, uneasy feeling that your first brain in your skull takes time to analyze and think about.

I had lots and lots of "gut" feelings about the relationship that developed into my twenty-one year marriage before it even got to deeper intimacy of any kind. I did get that sick feeling inside; I did get a sense of dread or foreboding; I did have the urge to get away; I did want to get out.

But what kept me in? Something other than what my gut was saying or my brain might have been thinking. It was deep and psychological and even spiritual. Initially I did develop the "behavioral inaction" of doing nothing, because I was so shocked when he first started cursing at me that I did not know what to do. I had grown up in an abusive and strange adoptive home where my adoptive parents told me I was a mistake to have been adopted and I had been beaten and hit and cursed at up until the age of fifteen when I left to live on my own. By the time I was in my mid-twenties I had already been rejected by the man whom I thought was my "soul mate" and "true love" so I was already emotionally jaded, jilted and vulnerable when my abuser appeared on the scene.

In some ways I was pre-programmed for abuse as an adult because I had been so shredded by abuse as a child. It really did have a lot to do with an unstable sense of self-esteem and I took this with me full steam ahead into the vortex of the abuse into which I found myself sucked.

It also had to do with my spiritual state of affairs. Because I did not end up marrying the man whom I had loved since I was eighteen, I felt I had to grab what I could, because by the time I got involved with the man who eventually became my legal husband I was twenty-six and feeling very old—especially since I had been on my own since I was fifteen. I remember saying to God, *"I don't care, I am going to do this anyway, since you did not give me what I wanted I am going to take this. I don't care what happens down the road."* There were ministers and friends who told me the relationship was bad, and I did not listen. I had my gut, the experience of abuse with him before we married, the advice of friends, and my own intelligence, and yet I chose to marry a man who had already cursed at me, put me down, tried to control me, and physically assaulted me. I was a smart woman who had made a very foolish choice. By then I honestly did feel that perhaps this was all I was worth, that I must really be an unworthy person deserving of such a man, or God would have brought me something better. And since He didn't (so the logic went), I grabbed this horrid thing in my desperation, and I spent twenty-three years in much misery, unhappiness, regret and ultimately, a complete mental breakdown, from which I am still recovering.

As we look at the phases of the abuse cycle in Chapter Five, I urge you to use that gut of yours, and the advice of others, and even your own logic, and try to see what the true scenario is rather than what the abuse is beginning to tell you or your delusions are duping you into seeing. I guarantee you that being single and alone without abuse is infinitely better than settling for what has already begun to scar you and destroy you. Pull away, step back, look at it, think, think and think again. Even if it is stepping into the unknown or facing great fears or loneliness or abandonment or the fear of not having kids or whatever else is keeping you in this relationship, it will come to nothing but despair and ruin of your psyche from which it is very difficult to recover, and which sometimes can be fatal, if you remain.

# CHAPTER FOUR: PHASES IN THE ABUSE PROCESS: FROM NICE TO NO WAY OUT

*Warning: This chapter contains offensive language and describes sexual abuse. It is meant to show the realities of abuse. It is not condoning the language or the actions of abuse. Please use discretion when using this material. Please note that the phases delineated are not hard and fast, may overlap, regress, skip, or occur concurrently, because each situation of abuse is unique.*

## PHASE ONE: SO BEGUILING

At first he seems so nice, so sweet, generous and sincere. Don't you feel flattered when he buys you that nice gold necklace, even if it means he can't pay his rent that month? And even if it made you feel a little uncomfortable at first, weren't you at least flattered by his saying "I love you" only a short time after you started dating? He certainly has a way with words, he is so "sweet-talking" and it comes on fast and he says so much so soon. You get so caught up in the excitement of it all.

*What he says does not immediately betray who he is.* Abusers are sly, suave, cunning, generally intelligent (though not necessarily well-educated), enticing, seductive. What lies underneath the sugar-coated words is an insect waiting to trap its prey, an organism which needs to feed off of vulnerability, like a spider in its web or a Venus fly trap. Each uses some vulnerability of the unsuspecting prey to lure them to their demise, and they enjoy every minute that the web tangles them in or the juices digest the creature alive.

This is what they feed off of— your vital energy, which they gorge on because you are still alive and fighting as they do it.

*You are attracted because you are somehow vulnerable.* Are you naive? Have you had much experience in love? Are you young? Are you insecure? Are you prone to liking flattery? Are you just plain horny? Or lonely? An abuser will hone in on any of the vulnerabilities, just like tigers and lions and cheetahs in the wild do not attack the fastest and the most able of the animals they are stalking, but the one with a lame leg, or who is sick, or who is young, or who is lost, or separated from the pack.

*He seems intensely interested in you, and you get taken in by it.* When you share your liking for a particular author or composer or music group or movie or TV show, be sure he is going to mirror you and is going to love what you love, even if he has never read that novel or watched that TV show before. Does he have any interests that are not exactly like yours, does he tell you about them before you tell him about yours? Notice whether he is mirroring because this is another form of ensnarement.

*He tickles your fancy.* Does he tell you urgently how beautiful you are, how much you mean to him, how quickly he wants to move things forward (sexually or perhaps in engagement or marriage)? Beware, because an abuser does not want you to really know him before you get entangled. He wants to hide and obscure his perhaps criminal background, drug abuse, previous abusive relationships, habits and proclivities from you. The goal is to achieve intimacy without ever reaching the trueness in either of you. This way, he can claw and grab and ensnare before you have had a chance to figure out who he is, and before the damaging effects of abuse demoralize you and change how you react to things. It may seem like he is so quickly committed because he wants an "old-fashioned relationship", but to him this ultimately means one in which he can vicariously punish females in anger and use them as a stepping stool to stand, chest outward and pounding it, in asserting his deficient sense of power and control. Beware, beware of the push, of the quickness, of the urgency to move forward!

## PHASE TWO: MOST CRITICAL: A PEEK INTO HIS PAST AND YOUR FUTURE

After some time, do you notice he begins to have a short fuse at you? Does he begin to yell about anything, curse, throw something, or get angry at external factors, usually ones beyond his control? Does he get a speeding ticket and blame the cop? Are you late coming home, and does he start getting short with you about it? Does he start cursing when you never heard him curse before? Does he blame his employer if he has a problem on the job? Did he raise his voice at you for taking too long to call him or leaving dishes in the sink?

You can give all kinds of excuses for this, but I would say that this is the critical phase where he will begin to test you, to see what you will take from him, how much, in what quantities and in what duration. "It's just a phase," you say. "He's just touchy today." "You know how sensitive he is." "He's in a bad mood!" "Maybe he did not have enough today (sleep, caffeine, sex)." You have to understand that he needs a living entity to suck on, to draw his life from, because he has at the same time no real identity and yet an over-inflated ego and narcissistic character, that will perceive the wrongs of the world as coming from everywhere but him— you included. It will not be long before he starts to show you his world view. Watch! Listen! Observe!

Even the smallest thing which shocks you, or hurts you, or perturbs you, is a warning sign. Do not underestimate it! Understand also that you can dismiss these early signs as part of his 0temperament, or his hard day at work, or his nationality or race, or his health. None of these is true, and if you take this route you begin the rationalization process that starts the entanglement of abuse. If you excuse him then you give him the excuse to abuse you, and once you get in, it becomes difficult to get out and in some cases fatally impossible. If even the slightest things starts to irk you, no matter how good he may make you otherwise feel, check yourself, stop, do your research, hold back, wait, abstain, withdraw, consider, reconsider, ask advice, research, but do not move forward.

Looking back at the earliest phases of my relationship with the abuser who became my "husband" of twenty-one years, I can see that the warning signs were there, but I ignored them. Here were mine, the ones I ignored to my own destruction:

He began cursing, first in general, and then at me. I thought it was part of his "cocky" personality— sort of the "bad boy" guy that had a history but was trying to change and merely showed residual traits from his past. I think the first time he cursed at me he said bitch or fucking bitch to me and I remember I froze with fear. Did he really just say that? What did I do? He can't really mean that! I remember standing there paralyzed and wondering what this really meant. Wasn't he a Christian? Why would he say this to me? I was frightened and on alert. And I believe I went along for a bit longer, until I tried to get away the first time.

And over the years, I was called everything horrid and degrading to a female: cunt, whore, fucking cunt, fucking whore, piece of shit, fat ass, fat whale, fat fucking bitch, lazy fat fucking bitch , and various permutations of this. I can tell you that being called these things after bearing this man his children caused more wounding to me than all the times he hit me, or threw something at me, or threw me into something, or threatened to kill me, or tried to kill me. Cursing is definitely a signal that something is wrong and going very wrong in your relationship. Consider this as a primary flag and get out before you hear years of worse things said to you.

He gave me double messages. Here was a man who claimed to be a Christian, who was able to praise his God with one breath and then curse about something the next. Here was a man who once had told me he had been addicted to heroin, but drank enough beer to be more than casual or social drinking. He would tell me he could "handle his alcohol" and it became difficult for me to know whether that was true or not. He said that he wanted to be a "Christian" man but seemed to be wanting to fight with everyone and everything around him— church leaders, cops, the IRS, the "government," and me.

He told me about his past, but I did not take it seriously enough. Here was a man who unlike some abusers did tell me what I needed to know: 1. he had had a serious, debilitating heroin habit and had been a drug dealer until supposedly some years before I met him 2. he had been in jail for tying up an elderly woman in order to steal money and jewelry from her 3. his former girlfriend told one of his sisters that she "never, ever wanted to see him again" 4. he had never filed an income tax return and he was twenty-nine years old 4. he falsified his name by changing one letter and/or one number on tax forms in order to obscure his identity 5. he "use to beat up gay guys" when he was a teenager 6. he expressed anti-Semitism and used to harass an old Jewish man he knew by holding up a bagel at him and shouting "BAGEL! BAGEL!" 7. having used the services of prostitutes. 8. having an intense hatred of his mother, while having an unrealistic, idealistic view of his alcoholic, abusive father, who left his mother with seven children to raise alone.

I have said of our relationship, "He was horny; I was desperate." I look back to the very early days of the relationship and I had more than enough warning signs that this was a bad thing and I should have gotten out. In fact, I did try to get out several times before succumbing to my own desperation and not only returning to him, but marrying him.

I felt this was the best I was going to get. Perhaps of all the warning signs this was the one I should have heeded the most. By the time I married I was twenty-seven years old. In New York City terms this is not particularly young or old to marry, but I had been on my own since I was fifteen and so I was feeling pretty old by that point. I suppose I really did feel my biological clock ticking. I had a slew of relationships that went nowhere and one that had really broken my heart. So perhaps I gained a certain nihilism about life and felt that this was going to be my lot. What else was I going to find? I probably will never get married if I don't marry him. I felt that if I didn't take the chance at this man's penis and his sperm, I would never have children.

I chose to marry an abuser because I was abused as a child. It is painful to admit this but there is a certain "learned helplessness" or resignation that one learns from being abused as a child. Maybe I really am the things they said I was. My adoptive father told me I was a "little piece of shit" and besides the many times he hit me with various objects, he said that the worst thing he and my adoptive mother ever did was adopt me. Maybe I really am what they said I am? It is difficult to admit that I let some of those recordings play when my abuser began to do the same sorts of things to me that my adoptive father had done. I relate the entirety of my failed adoption experience and why I left home at fifteen in my book *When Adoption Fails*.

Were you abused as a child? Have you had a previous abusive partner? You will have to take a cold and hard look at yourself and see that you are already "pre-programmed" as it were, to choose another abusive relationship. If there is any way you can get to a counselor or an abuse support group and discuss what is going on, and try to get out even though you somehow feel what you are in is familiar and comfortable, you can avoid long term trauma, damage and even death and the hands of another abuser. I believe it is at this earliest warning stage that getting out is the easiest to do, but the subtlety of the abuser's craft will make being able to make proper discernment difficult. I do understand this. But see as we progress here how the next phase spirals into something that is even more difficult to escape from and how great is the debilitation and degradation that occurs once the abuser begins to really feed upon your life and soul and spirit.

PHASE THREE: THE ABUSE BEGINS; THE WEB GETS STICKY

He starts to reveal his true colors to you. Those explosive episodes or being pissed off at you or everyone else devolves into put-downs, insults, spying, false accusations, intimidation, threats and sexual coercion. If you show any resistance or feistiness or courage be prepared for a backlash. He is tangling you in the web and trying to get you to try so hard that the threads tighten even harder and ultimately wear out your strength. If you have anything left of yourself at this phase, run screaming if you have to, but run away and don't come back! No matter how you feel and what still attracts you!

I remember when I was at this phase of the relationship and it was then that I really should have gotten out and had opportunity to do so. During this "real abuse" period he punched me in my breast and I had him arrested, and got the first of my many protective orders against him. This was the first of many times I had seen him behind bars. I was to keep that order (as I did five others) for only a few months until I dropped it and continued on with the relationship.

I also remember having some kind of altercation with him, and as I was getting into my car to drive away, he sat on top of the car and prevented me from driving it. It may have been the same day, or a different day, but I also remember him opening up the hood of my car and taking some wires or something out so I could not drive it. I also remember at this stage that I woke up to find he had scaled the walls of the farmhouse I was living in and had climbed through the second floor window to the foot of my bed and stood there over me as I woke.

I think out of all the experiences I had up until that point this one might be have the one to do me in. I could not fight that kind of strength! What else could he do? Maybe I should take the path of least resistance? Something solidified in me over that experience, a real sense of fatalism and "learned helplessness."

I was hiding how bad it was from people. I wanted so much to get married and have children that I compromised everything about myself to achieve it— my career, my talents, my sensitivities, my sense of worth (if I had any), my faith, my habits, my sense of security. I did not really explain it as fully as I should have at the time to the people closest to me. I would say things like "we have had some rough spots but we are working on it." It was during this period where the abuse began to blossom that I actually married him. And I remember my first child, my oldest daughter, sitting upright on the bed, at the age of about nine months, watching as he threw my body and my head onto the floor in front of her, and what I was thinking as he hurt me. *"He will stop before she is old enough to remember this, I am sure he will."* How cruelly untrue this turned out to be, for all six of my children! You can have various thoughts during this phase. *"We can work this out;" "God can change anyone;" "I am human, too; I also make mistakes;" "There is hope for a future, we have time;" "He really isn't always this way;" "After all, when we are in public he is different;" "It really must be a phase;" "Well, he really was traumatized as a child."* It is all rot and rubbish and crap and deception and unreality.

One of the most perplexing things about my abuser was his "double personality"— how he could behave a certain way in certain public situations but be an entirely different person in private with me. It was countless times that he would be cursing and hollering at me on the way to church, and then as soon as we sat down it in the pew, it was "Praise God" and "Halleluiah!" His initial, most superficial personality, what Freud would call his superego or his public persona, is one that is affable, and congenial, and friendly—

almost overly friendly, sincerely saccharine-sounding and earnest-sounding. It was not conceivable to many people that I was dealing with such a wretched condition outside of church walls. In fact, even when we had guests in our home he acted fairly okay— so there was a point where I preferred having company around because at least he was on better behavior and I could survive it.

Why didn't I get out sooner, even if I married him? That is the question. I remember three weeks after our marriage he was not coming home at night, and I found him in a dark, smelly, drug and beer-infested lair with some of his friends. During that same early marriage period I found him at a bar in the area and chased him outside the bar because I was trying to take the car keys from him. I ended tripping on a metal stake that was sticking up in the yard and have a large scar on my foot to this day from it. "How did you get that cut on your foot, m'am?" "Oh, chasing my drunk husband around the streets to take his keys, because I didn't want him to drive." Nice emergency room talk for a newlywed!

I also got pregnant three months after I got married. Be careful what you wish for. I remember even before getting pregnant saying "I should get an annulment; I honestly thought he was someone else and I have been deceived about him" but then I stood between this very hard rock and this very hard place: if I divorce this man I may never have children. So yes, I did chose the penis and the sperm and I did have my children— all six of them. And it took me twenty-three years to finally get out of the situation and I today I am finally and fully free from his abuse. Not free, however, from the memories and not the effects that it still has on my children today— but away from him forever, I finally and fully did that. I would rather be dead than have to ever be near him or see him again.

It was this early in the relationship that not only had the physical abuse begun, but that he began demeaning my physical appearance as a means of subjection and domination and control. By all standards I have been considered a beautiful woman— he even said that he thought I was the most beautiful woman he had ever seen. Most of my life I have worn my long, relatively straight hair unstyled but groomed. And then I remember him one day in the early marriage period— out of the blue— saying "Why don't you do something with your hair? You look like a scarecrow." I should have laughed at it and told him to screw himself, but somehow it all irked me and degraded me and took something away from me. Later on, he used to call me "fat fuck"— this was after having five of the six children I bore him— before that point I had pretty well kept my weight reasonable, considering that for five full years of my life I was pregnant (and some of those months both pregnant and breastfeeding at the same time), twelve full years of my life I was breastfeeding, and I had had six children by the time I was thirty-eight. So I remember him calling me "fat fuck" and "fat bitch" and "fat cow"" and "lard ass"", and then I finally said "Fat? You wanna see FAT?" And I ate an entire tub of Haagen- Daz ice cream. I ate with abandon after that. I was fat, right? It just didn't matter anymore. And for the last fifteen years I have struggled with my weight, with diets and exercise and the weight-gaining side-effects of medications.

Besides the put-downs and cursing and insults the worst part of this phase is the unveiling of threats. Threats are used to control the victim and keep them with the abuse through fear and intimidation. He may threaten you with bodily harm: "I am going to throw you down the stairs;" he may threaten to take away your children: "I will drive away in the middle of the night and you will never see the kids again;" he may threaten to ruin your life and reputation: "I will call Children and Youth Services on you and report you as a horrible mother;" or "I will have you committed to a mental hospital and then I will take the kids from you;" threats of withholding financial support: "If you leave me and try to get child support, I will disappear and the kids will never see me again, and you will never get a penny from me."

If you have had children with an abuser, or have had children with someone else and then end up with an abuser, the threat of being separated from your children, having your children taken from you, or having no means of support can be terrifying and can be enough to keep you from trying to get free. Sometimes you cannot see that the threats are spurious and without power. They are more like "that man behind the curtain" who turns out to be the Wizard that you thought was "the Great and All-Powerful Oz." Many women in abusive situations simply do not have the financial means to make it without what support they might get from the abuser, but the scenario (as it took me too long to find out) is that eventually you will make it without him, but you might have a very rough year or so until you get on your feet. I encourage you, do not let fear of finances keep you in abuse! Better to be a little poorer and a lot freer, than kept in bondage!

## PHASE FOUR: GETTING WORSE AND NEW WAYS OF COPING

In this phase we are talking about threats of violence and all-out physical violence. Some women do not survive this phase. I read all too often of a man who shoots a woman in the face, pours acid on a woman, rapes and kills and mutilates a woman, sets fire to a woman, strangles a woman, stabs and slices a woman and drowns a woman. The first act of physical abuse upon me was being punched in the breast, and the last act of physical abuse upon me was being punched in the breast. In between my head was thrown into the sharp point of a cedar chest, my leg was wedged and slammed between a car door, I was choked from behind while driving on the highway, was thrown head first onto the floor, was punched in the head, was punched in the solar plexus, was kicked in my vagina, was thrown into things, was bruised, was coerced into sex, and other things I cannot remember. I was threatened with being thrown down a flight of stairs and being drowned in a lake and thrown off a third-story balcony. There are women who have had it way harder than I have had it in this regard. I cannot imagine broken bones and disfigured bodies and faces but this has happened to many a woman. I did have my share, but I know many have had it far worse. You may be hit, kicked, punched, thrown, slapped, twisted, crushed, choked, stabbed, burned, poisoned, drowned or shot.

The level of control will increase at this stage. If he really has gotten a hold of you, he will be able to restrict whom you talk to, who visits you, where you go, what you do, what money you have and spend, what you do with your time, what you eat, and if it is worse than anything, how you pray and how you think. You have to wonder why so many people who get involved in cults are similar in outcome to victims of abuse and domestic violence. To make it worse (or perhaps just to be a prick) he might even try to disturb your sleep by waking you up and night for no apparent reason. Sleep deprivation is a tactic used in mind control scenarios.

The worst perhaps is sexual abuse. You may think (and worse, he may think) that being married or being committed means he can take sex from you whenever he wants it, but anytime a person forces sex upon you it is an act of rape, and there is not an iota of love or beauty in rape. This is not love-making but an act of violence. It can often start with requests, sometimes to explore what you might consider to be perverse or unusual sex practices or positions. When you say no or say you are not comfortable with these requests you will get a load of intimidation and manipulation, because a stiff penis knows no bounds if it pokes out of a determined abuser. He will plead and implore and whine with "please"s and "come on"s and "why not"s. After all, if you love him, you want him to be satisfied, right? Obviously you are not a good wife or girlfriend or partner if you don't do what he wants! If you do not give in to one thing you will probably end up settling for something else, sometimes just to get him off your back, literally. And sometimes you might wake to find he is starting sex on you or with you in your sleep, which without your volition is a violation, an act of rape.

When it comes to sex, abusers can be very possessive. You are their object, their possession, their orgasm maker, their semen conduit, their unpaid prostitute, their hole— all under the guise of how much they "love" you. But remember, he will tell you soon enough that you "belong to him" and that your vagina and breasts are "his property" and that if you do not give him what he wants, it must be because you are getting it somewhere else. Along with the sexual possessiveness comes suspicions of infidelity, or even homosexuality. If you do want to have sex with him, then you obviously have a lover, or you are a lesbian!

Ironically, it is often when you start to loathe his company and his presence and his body that he begins to accuse you of these things, but his narcissism prevents him from realizing that the fault is with them and not with you. I used to tell my abuser that if he wanted sex so much, he can go to the store and get two pieces of liver, because I was just a piece of meat to him anyway. I never felt loved or respected or cherished or valued or protected or appreciated or fulfilled or satisfied in my sex life with my abuser, except on the most basic level of orgasm, and the fact that through his sperm I became a mother.

He will destroy your property. If he cannot or will not hurt you for whatever reason, he can hurt your things. Your possessions are a vicarious means of hurting and even killing you. When my abuser's father was being evicted from his home for his own violence against my abuser's mother, he cut up all her clothes and laid them on the bed. My abuser smashed our daughter's cellphone into a brick fireplace. He threw my stainless steel wok off a third-story balcony. He broke numerous dishes and picture frames and fragile items. He disabled my car so I could not drive it.

He may even spy on you. In the case of Nicole Brown Simpson and OJ Simpson, which I cover in Chapter Six, you will see how OJ spied on Nicole through a window when she was engaging in sex with other men, and this fueled his jealous rage and gave him a reason for his vengeful violence against her, by which he murdered her. It is truly animalistic nature at its best! He may also spy on your phone calls, text messages, social networking and email accounts, bank statements even at your place of employment or school. If spying behavior appears earlier in the relationship than this phase— as early as the beginning or phase two—all the more reason to read the warning signs and get away before he entangles you!

What do you do if you have reached this unfortunate stage without being able to get out? You begin to think that maybe you do need to call that domestic violence hotline, or tell your pastor, or even get a protective order. "If I tell anyone, they won't believe me." Or maybe you develop a perverted sense of relief after each assault. "Thank God nobody can see this injury." "It's really not that big a bruise." Or avoidance. "I need to lay down." "If I just forget about it then it will go away." Then again, signs of trying to get out are coming clear: "I took pictures of my injury." Or, a perverting of the thought processes: "Maybe I am not submissive enough."

And on the issue of "submission", I would say that within many groups (religious and non-religious) is the issue of one person or people being "submissive" to another person. I have found particularly in male/female relationships that abusers will use the umbrella of religion to either find a mate he can ensnare or keep one ensnared once he finds her. This is a serious evil and I know there are many women from "religious" communities who are being hurt and raped and threatened and demoralized by a man who claims his "religion" allows him to treat her the way he does. Nothing is more perverse than this to me and I hope that what I am saying here will help many women ensnared in abuse to break free before the entanglement destroys them.

I say this because I, too, thought that perhaps I was not "submissive enough" and that perhaps the problems in my marriage were due to my not being submissive enough. "If I do the changing, then he will change, because the problem is with me." I found some religious teachings which seemed to imply that any problems in a marriage was the fault of the woman, and desperate as I was to do anything to get relief from my bondage I tried being "submissive." This ended up with our moving thousands of miles to a religious community that among other things espoused submission of the woman to the man virtually unconditionally. In some cases I believe abuse was happening to other women but it was tightly closeted and even tacitly accepted as part of the "submissive" role espoused by the community.

And what happened was that the more "submissive" I became to him, the more abusive he became to me. I do not think the submissive woman/loving man paradigm works in cases of abuse, if it does at all in this modern age. This just gives the sociopathic, narcissistic bully-abuse-personality-type male a field day with any vulnerable woman who believes these teachings. Whatever the Bible teaches on the subject of male/female relations and husband-wife relations, I know that what I lived was not good or right or healthy or beautiful or wondrous or happy or holy or godly. And the veil of male domination made it even easier for my abuser to continue to abuse me with impunity in the name of religion.

After a number of years in that community I pulled away. It took me another ten years to finally divorce my abuser and two years after that to get final protective order and cease all contact with him. If you do find things have gotten this far, it is not too late to try to get away. I will go over techniques for getting away in Chapter Nine.

## PHASE FIVE: CRISIS PROPORTIONS AND NEW LIFE SKILLS

By this point he has trained you to react. He is getting comfortable with his victories. He will get threatened if you stand up and will retaliate if you stand up— physically, financially, psychologically, socially, even religiously. The violence is more pointed, if not more frequent. By now you have been thoroughly indoctrinated into your abuser's one-person cult, and you believe the situation is your fault. He continues to make threats or act out. The threats may now escalate to threats of death.

You have to strategize in order to survive, so you develop new ways of thinking and surviving, some of which conflict with each other and reflect your state of constant flux. "I will be more submissive." *"He will be better if I give him more sex." "I will fight back." "I will stand up." "I will not stand up." "I will ignore this." "I will tell people." "I will not tell people." "This is what I deserve."* And most tellingly, *"This is my life now."*

This is a critical state where you may start manifesting health problems such as sleep disorder, anxiety, depression, fibromyalgia, asthma, gastrointestinal disorders, palpitations, high blood pressure, social withdrawal, mental breakdown. You have been figuring out what you need to do to survive. You may have tried a protective order or separation, but his honey-coated words of contrition and repentance caused you to go back. You have been conditioned to believe staying in the situation is better for the children than being the victims of divorce. If you have actually taken the step to separate or get a PFA, he may back down a bit and be willing to go for counseling. It may be too little, too late, or an exercise in futility, but you will discover new levels of his perversity when you meet with a professional counselor or minister.

## PHASE SIX: COUNSELING

This really is a great ride. Wait until you see an Academy Award-winning performance of such innocence and sense of indignation! The poor guy, you have said such nasty things about him! You have made people think bad things about him! You have talked about to other people! How dare you!

When confronted with the scenarios that you inevitably describe to the third party, you can expect the poor wounded soul to come ferociously to his own defense. "She deserved it after what she did!" "I didn't do anything!" "You would get mad too if you lived with her!" "She's crazy!" "She is a bad wife/mother!" "She is mentally imbalanced!" "She clearly is lying!" "She is exaggerating!" "I barely brushed her skin!" "I didn't force myself on her, I was just trying to get her excited!" "I only touched her a little!" "I only brushed my hand against her head!" "She fell onto the edge of the table, I did not push her!" "Well, you know, I said I was sorry."

Of course you have your own version of things, which may sound problematic in and of themselves if they were not heard in the context of abuse. *"Of course I go off the handle after what he does!" "Of course I am depressed!" "Of course I might need a drink!" "Of course I might need Ativan or Valium!"* And then when you get home, you start to think differently, because things have calmed down a bit and he is so repentant. *"Maybe I did set him off." "I want to keep going for the sake of the kids."* *"He was really nice for a few days afterward."* And maybe he was, because that is the nature of the cycle of abuse. But as the sun rises so it will cycle again and he will abuse you again.

## PHASE SEVEN: THE LAW

There are different ways that the law can be brought into an abusive relationship. It might be because someone heard or saw you arguing or fighting and they called the police to your home. It might be because he hit you or hurt you and you reacted and called the police or someone in your home called the police. It might be because something happened in a public place and someone else called the police to the scene. It might be that you decided to get an order of protection. That will involve going before a judge, which will also happen if separate charges are brought against him for harassment or assault or even attempted murder in worst case scenarios. A lawyer may also be brought into the situation in the case of protective orders (in our county it is through an agency that provides free legal representation to victims of abuse). A lawyer may also be called upon to represent in custody and child support issues if you get to the point of separation or divorce. In all these cases, once things get bad with an abuser, expect to see police officers, judges and lawyers in your life, probably repeatedly and for many years to come. In the cases where there are other criminal charges, you may also expect to have interactions with probation officers, especially if you abuser breaks a protective order or commits other crimes while he is on probation.

Something initially happens to get the law involved. What did he do to you, and what did you do about it, or someone else do about it? This is where the law gets involved. Unless you call or someone else calls, the police will not know what happened to you. Unless you file for a protective order (and this you have to do yourself) no one is going to know in the legal system what is going on with you. So something gets the ball rolling. If someone else calls, you may be so frightened of the situation that you will lie to the police officers when they show up. "Everything is fine, Officer; we just had a little squabble." "No he did not hurt me." "No, everything is all right." (Notice the reaction of your abuser if one of the officers is a female. One woman with a gun outpowers any man without one, which is very disconcerting indeed to the abusive disposition.) And his words may also obfuscate the truth of what is going on: "She is lying, Officer, I swear I did not hit her!" "She is just out to get me!" "She is just jealous because she thinks I have a girlfriend on the side!" "She made all of this up!" "I did not threaten her or hold her over the balcony!" "She just wants my money, Officer, that's all this is about!" "She drove me to it, she provoked me!"

He may have threatened you before the cops came with worse harm if you dare say anything about what happened. You may also be intrinsically afraid because once the cops leave you will be alone with him and have to face what he may say and do next. The result of such an interaction may be several things. Nothing may happen and the police will leave— although be aware that a record is kept that they were called. Your abuser may face a disorderly conduct charge or assault or battery charge or worse. He can be arrested. You can be taken aside and counseled to get a protective order. He may be forced to leave the domicile, or you may be encouraged to leave the domicile.

All of this in actuality does not bode well for the woman living in fear of a bully and a coward. Imagine what is going through the mind of the abuser. "How dare she call the cops on me!" "I am going to make sure she never does that again!" "She ain't seen nothing yet" "That bitch!" "She lied to them about what happened!" "She made me do it anyway!" "Just wait until we are alone!" "She won't be able to prove anything next time, I will be sure of that!" "She will be sorry she ever said a word to those pigs!" And what is going through your own mind? "I am afraid of what he will do to me"; "He doesn't always do this"; "I don't want him to get into trouble"; "I don't want him to do something to me in revenge"; "I just want him to stop."

The situation can thus devolve and it is for this reason that many women do not call when they are injured or threatened. On the outside, it looks stupid and weak and self-defeating. But if you are living with the fear of reprisal, one is seriously constrained from doing anything that could possibly make the situation worse.

## PHASE EIGHT: ATTEMPTING TO GET OUT

Imagine being afraid to do something because someone could hurt you or kill you if you did it. Imagine being afraid to do something because your children could disappear if you did it. Imagine being afraid to do something because it feels that life may be worse if you did than if you didn't.

And so it is when a woman contemplates leaving an abusive relationship. There is so much to consider, so much to fear! *What if I leave, will he harass me where I am going? Will he bother me at work? Will he spy on me? Will he hurt me? Will he follow through with his threats? Will he try to kidnap the kids? Will he call Children and Youth Service on me out of spite? Will he refuse to give me any money? Will he break into my home? Will he turn the kids against me? Will he accuse me of being unfaithful to him? Will I be able to manage the situation alone? Will I have enough money to make it through? Don't the children still need a father? What will he try to do that I have not anticipated? What will he do to me? How can I ever get out of this situation?*

And imagine me, a woman who had no money of her own, no parents or family to help, no religious community who took the situation seriously enough, no place nearby to go, with an increasingly-large family, trying to earn money as best as she could, getting two college degrees, homeschooling and trying not to go insane. There is every reason why you should leave the abusive situation and many reasons why you cannot.

In Chapter Five I cover what you can do if you cannot get out and in Chapter Eight I cover the whole issue and process of the protective order, custody, child support, counseling, and other mechanics by which you can endeavor to be free from your abusive situation. But suffice it to say here, that every woman who makes an attempt to flee is a heroine, and the deeper you have become entrapped by the vortex the harder it is going to be to emerge on the other side.


PHASE NINE: THE CYCLE OR YOUR FREEDOM?

The situation is what it is, then it gets really bad, then it gets horrible, then it gets dangerous, then some crisis happens and it reaches some kind of climax, and then it seems to resolve temporarily and fade into false flaccidity. Such is the cycle of abuse, like a perverse orgasm that needs to build and rise and thrust and explode and then heaves slower and slower until the unquiet calm is reached and the rush is needed again. It is more like this than the gentle ebb and flow of the tide or the cycles of the moon.

All too often the abusive victim becomes ensnared in the cycle drama until she loses her will to fight back or learns exceedingly well how to adapt. As a species we do well when we adapt. It is partially for this reason that the cycle continues over and over, for some into years or a lifetime of suffering and some in murder and death.

And then you reach out your hand into the unknown, full of fear and anxiety because you are not sure how you could make it if you tried. Sometimes there really is a lack of extrinsic support, sometimes you make excuses why you cannot do it. Sometimes you do not even try. Sometimes you try and fail.

But I will say to all who are still in the cycle, that you can get out of cycle, and that you can be free. I wish I had made better choices earlier on and spared my children and myself much suffering. I wish I had been braver and I wish I had not been so afraid of the unknown. I wish that I had not listened to the lies and threats of my abuser and believed them. I wish I had not lived in such a sense of resignation and futility. I lost so much of my self-esteem and purpose and this kept me in bondage so much longer than I should have ever been. I could have taken the plunge into that unknown a lot sooner and been done with this horrid mess I created many years before I finally was done with it. But each of you can get out sooner than I did and I want you to go for it.

In the following chapter I discuss what you can do when can't get out, or perceive that you cannot get out, or are in the process of getting out.

# CHAPTER FIVE: WHAT TO DO WHEN YOU CANNOT GET OUT

*"Domestic violence is one of the most chronically under-reported crimes."*— U.S. Department of Justice 2003
*"Eventually, the continued abuse wears down the victims so much that they are unable to leave due to physical and mental exhaustion. The men gradually take control of the womens' psyches and destroy their ability to think clearly. The women come to believe they deserve the abuse and that they are incompetent."*— Elaine Carmen, MD

I do understand that you cannot get out. That it feels that you cannot get out. That you are afraid of trying to get out. That you tried and failed to get out. That you have given up on getting out. Or even that you do not feel the need to get out right now.

## TO THOSE ON THE OUTSIDE LOOKING IN

To those on the outside of abuse I know it seems like weakness or foolishness on the part of the victim to stay in a situation of abuse. You may have heard the fights and arguments. You may have seen the injuries. You may have listened as she cried to you on the phone or sent those horrid emails. You may have held her as she wept. You may have gotten into an argument with the abuser yourself, or even called the police on him. So in a sense, if you have done any of these things you are in "insider" in the abuse situation and you are perhaps intimately connected with the sufferings of your friend, sister, cousin, niece, co-worker, daughter, or mother. The frustration for you must be immense. Why is she being so foolish? She's being an idiot. He is not worthy of her. He is a real scumbag, of course she should get away. Why does she keep on going back to him, even when she has had him arrested and had a protective order? Why did I give her money to help her leave and now she is back with him? It seems like a waste. She is doing more harm to her kids staying with him than leaving, can't she see that? She is stronger than she thinks she is. What is wrong with her? Why can't she make a plan and stick to it? What attracts her to that guy anyway? I am tired of hearing her merry-go-round stories. It's the same thing over and over again. I don't even know what to say to her anymore.

Those on the outside cannot really know how horrible it is living in abuse, unless you have lived through it yourself, and even then it can get frustrating to see the person you care about going through something you went through and see her keep going back to it or staying in it.

Well brava to you, that you yourself were able to get out, if you are a woman who has gotten out of an abusive relationship or marriage. It took every ounce of your will to do it. You pushed through your fear of the unknown. You reached out help and availed yourself of resources. You managed to make it through and start over.

But for many women in abuse, the road to disentanglement may take longer and the stickiness of the situation may entrap her harder or differently. I do know that the most compassion I have received over my abusive marriage came from people in my life who also had suffered abuse—my birth mother, and two of my best friends. In fact, I believe it was destiny, or the will of God, that I met and had a close ten-year friendship with a younger woman whom I helped with her situation and the mechanics of a protective order and divorce and finally getting free.

## WHY ARE YOU STILL THERE?

The reasons are often layered and complex. I have felt every one of these and lived through every one of them. I do not judge your staying in and I applaud every thought you have had about leaving and every small or large attempt you have made to get away. But breaking down the reasons why you are still in it may aid a bit in understanding and giving you strength to carry on. Not every woman in abuse will have the same reasons for staying, but this is a panorama of possible motivations or realities. You may find resonance in one or more or all of these scenarios.

*Every act of abuse will condition you for more abuse.* This is a very hard reality, but when someone you think you love, or you think loves you, hurts you, then somehow you think there is some rightness or justification in it. *"Maybe I deserved what he did." "Maybe I am as bad as he said I was." "I feel so horrible about myself now I don't see he point of trying anymore."*

*You develop a sense of "learned helplessness."* A fatalism develops where you don't see the point of trying anymore. *"This is who I am now." "This is the way life is now." "I made my bed and I have to lie in it." "I did this to myself."* You feel that feel that it is your fault and this is your destiny.

*There is also a sense of "learned hopefulness."* You can develop a sense of perverse optimism about the situation that is unattached to reality. *"It will not always be this way." "He will certainly change, he just needs time." "God can do miracles and I am hoping for one here." "Aren't Christians supposed to believe the best in people?" "It will be so great when we are a happy couple with happy children. "*

*You may have developed an attachment to your abuser.* In spite of the way he is treating you, you somehow get attached to him. You desire to please him. You might even look forward to his interactions. This is what is known as "Stockholm Syndrome," which is named after a phenomenon which occurred when a group of people were held hostage at a bank in Stockholm, Sweden. Against all outward sensibility these captives grew emotionally attached to their abusers and worried about them after they were released and tried hard to please them while in captivity. Particularly poignant examples of this were Elizabeth Smart, who spent nine months in abuse in captivity with a crazy man and woman and worried about them as they were arrested, and the three women in Cleveland who spent over ten years chained and abused and tortured in the same home and worried about their most evil and demented abuser when they were finally free.

The fact that you have become attached to your abuser can cause feelings of shame and you may not want to admit this to yourself. In nature it is the ability to adapt that enhances the chances for survival. I see Stockholm Syndrome as an adaptive and coping mechanism whereby the person being abused seeks to mollify or appease the abuser by siding with him, rather than fighting against him.

In some scenarios it actually does work to some extent and you may be able to stave off some attack or threat by siding with the abuser. This may also involve giving sex when you really do not want to, or actually learning to like sex when this "partner" repulses you and scares you. It actually takes a type of bravery to get to the point of siding with the abuser because it demonstrates how far you are willing to go to try to survive. You may not even know you are doing it. But it is a good thing to be aware of it, because you may also be masking the abuse and in the early stages especially you might be able to get free if you catch the fact that you are siding with him and try to see why. This would be another warning sign to look for that may aid in your getting free.

*You may actually "love him."* I suppose I thought I loved my abuser at one time. I felt a lot of feelings but was that love? Feeling horny or being emotionally needy can seem like love. Co-dependency can seem like love. Fantasy can seem like love. Rebounding can seem like love. Orgasm can even seem like love. Like I said in Chapter Four, the whirlwind nature of the early stages of an abusive relationship can engender such intensity of feelings that you may feel a lot of intensity and it may seem like love, but is it?

But maybe you really do love him. We do love people who do hurtful things to us sometimes. It hurts me that my children have picked up on much of their father's behaviors towards me, and have treated me badly— but I still do really love them. It hurt me that my friend married a man that I was sure was on his way to being an abuser— but I still do really love her. My adoptive mother left me without a penny when she died— but I still did really love her. The man that I was engaged to before I married my abuser broke my heart— not just when we were young, but when we got back together thirty years later— and I did still really love him.

But that does not mean you have to live with him. It does not mean that you have to live your life in fear of him. It does not mean that you live in a situation where you are demeaned by him or hurt by him. The reality is, inasmuch as you may really love him, and abuser does not really love you. An abuser is never showing love when he abuses. He may think he loves you, and worse, you may think he loves you. You probably do love him, but he does not love you, because he does not know what love is.

If you still love him, you can live separately from him and still love him, if that is your choice. But I think you will find, if you can get away, that what you thought was love on his part was abuse, and what you think is love on your part will blow away like the wind or die as if from a hard disease.

*The children.* Children are a motivating force for any mother, the most motivating force. So it is obviously difficult when you are trying to do the best for your children but you are not sure that leaving your abuser is the right thing to do as it concerns your children. You may be afraid of how you are going to provide for them financially. You may be concerned that your children might grow up in a broken home or without a proper father. You may be afraid that they will resent you for tearing up their home. You fear they may end up resenting you for putting their father in jail, or his being forbidden from returning to the home, should you get a protective order. You fear that if he were to live somewhere else he would take the opportunity to turn the children against you without your being there to defend yourself. You are afraid that were he to get into another relationship the person may not be a good influence on your children and you would not be able to protect them.

Worse yet, he may expose your children to vagaries of his lifestyle that you think would be harmful to them. Even worse, you may feel as part of your religious or other belief system that separation and/or divorce to be a great sin, and that to stay in the situation is pleasing to God or is morally right. It was probably this reason above all others that kept me with my abuser far longer that I should have stayed. Once children come into the picture the ability to get out of abuse becomes exponentially more difficult.

It was my choice initially to stay with my abuser once I had the opportunity to do so, and before I had children. It seemed that each time I was trying to get away, I got pregnant again. I was also part of a religious community that eschewed birth control and not only believed in large families, but in some quarters believed that every act of sex was meant for procreation, and that to interrupt the passage of sperm to ovum in any way is a great sin against God. I also would never have ended the life of any of my children in my womb, no matter what the circumstances, as I had once chosen to do as a teenager. So by the time I was thirty-eight I had six beautiful children and the most wretched travesty of a marriage. I was thrilled to be a mother and miserable that I was married to such a man.

But I want to assure you, that my children are better now that I am free, and it is an understatement to say I am better now that I am free. I am dealing with "residuals" of the relationship with my abuser, because the children have treated me with what I call "echoes" of their father, saying things that he said to me and treating me not unlike the way he treated me. It gets better the longer time passes. I am so grateful for this. But if you can get out sooner, that is less years they will spend listening to his cursing and putdowns of you, less years of them watching you get hurt and thinking that is normal, less years of your being unable to function well, less years of living in such dysfunction and tension.

A counselor recently said to me, "Theresa, as much as you love your children, you cannot keep them from all suffering in life." That was a bitter pill to swallow, but for some of you this might be a freeing concept. I wanted so very much to keep my children from suffering. No matter which way you go in an abusive relationship— staying or getting free— your children are going to suffer. It is obviously no fault of their own but they are going to suffer. But I can assure you that the suffering of growing up in a single parent household is preferable to suffering in a totally dysfunctional home with two parents. I guess on some level, I thought that separating from him was going to hurt them more than help them. I guess this was true when they were very young but maybe it was not true at all. I did not make my first major attempt to leave until my youngest of the six was a year old, which means my children were 1, 3, 5, 7, 9, and 11 when I went to a domestic violence shelter for the first and only time.

The children also will suffer from the effects of exposure to abuse. Things are quieter and less stressful now that I am free, but my children still mourn the loss of their father (from the divorce and protective order, but also from his chronic drug abuse), and their reactions to him range at this point to defensiveness on his behalf, matured concern, disinterest, baleful tears, and depression. These are sufferings I would have liked to have avoided for my children but you cannot expect them to grow up being exposed to such horrible things and it not take a toll on them somehow. It is my opinion now that getting out sooner— no matter how young the kids are or how bad you think it may be for them on whatever level— is decidedly preferable to staying in the abusive situation with your children. Although there are these emotional reasons for staying with an abuser if you have children, the fear of loss of financial support and your home is another factor in keeping you rather than getting you free.

*Fear of finances.* This one held me for a very long time. Part of the issue in my situation was that I hung on waiting for my adoptive mother to die, because when she died I was supposed to get a sizable inheritance and with it I was going to get away from my abuser and get a home of my own away from him and have no more financial worries. She died when my third child, my only son, was a year old, and I was disinherited upon her death, so I never did get the money. In retrospect I see that I married a man whose earnings and earning potential were unstable, but since I was going to get all that money someday I endured it with that long-term goal in mind. This was a lie and foolishness and poor judgment on my part. After this point I made some attempts to sing professionally again and then I began writing professionally and I created a home publishing business and then a natural wood blocks business and then I began teaching voice and then I taught music in a college and in a homeschool co-op and several community music schools, so you see I did try very hard over many years to help supplement my family's income.

But I was in a quandary when my kids were young, because I did firmly believe that I should be home with them and breastfeeding and practicing what is known as "attachment parenting," so I chose not to work outside the home other than the occasional singing gig. This is why I created my home-publishing business, so I could work from home while the children were young. Some of you might be able to avail yourself of the financial support of family members or of a generous and committed church or other organization. Some might have to resort to public welfare or going into a shelter before relocating into some kind of subsidized housing. In some cases you will be able to eventually get child support from the abuser. You may eventually be able to go to work if you are not working. Indeed these changes will be difficult and you will not have as much money in the short run and yes, things will be unstable in the interim and yes, there are worries about the future and yes, the neighborhood of the shelter may not be so great and yes, maybe you will have to move to a different school district and yes, there are myriad worries one can have, but I assure you, if you make the attempt to get out, the financial situation will eventually resolve, and the rewards of that far exceed the problems of monetary insecurity that you currently fear.

*Marriage as a "commitment."* This is a reason why many women in religious communities or of particular religious or cultural or moral persuasions stay in abusive marriages. Some religious women feel that the vows they made during their marriage ceremony absolutely create the marriage, and that to violate those vows would put their very salvation and eternal life in jeopardy. Some women come from cultures where divorce or even separation is frowned upon and viewed with disdain and derision. Some cultural groups actually view spousal abuse as an option and a right for the husband to exercise as he desires. Some feel that the institution of marriage needs to be upheld at all costs, to the detriment of society if it fails. I answer this by saying that if you are dead by the hand of your husband then you do not benefit society, if you live a lie then you cannot possibly be glorifying God, and that any society or culture or belief system that condones and perpetuates abuse of women is degraded and corrupt at its very core. You may have to face social ostracization and even danger for trying to leave and abusive husband, and I do acknowledge the real fear of retaliation or even death from some of the most severe scenarios.

*Fear of retaliation.* An abusive man who has his victim taken from him will often have his pride hurt and sense of security and control threatened, and will often wish to retaliate with vengeance against her. It has been noted that the period that is most dangerous to an abused woman is when she is actually trying to get out. These are very real fears and I do understand why for some women in some situations it is not possible to leave. I encourage you in this: that there may come a point when you might be able to leave, and that you should try with all your might if you feel you have as much chance dying if you stay as dying if you leave. You may have to resort to a complete relocation and the taking of another identity. You may have to go to that shelter and get that protective order. I understand that even with a protective order he can still get to you; the advantage of having one is that if he violates it (assuming he does not kill you in the process) he can be put in jail, which will leave you safe at least while he is incarcerated.

For some, his level of violence has not escalated to fear of serious injury or even bodily harm, but you never do know what level he will take it to next. This is why I encourage those of you in the early stages of an abusive relationship to utilize every resource you can to get out as early as you can. I think abusers are like animals that like the blood of a certain prey once they taste it. If you can get out early he may never get to take your blood.

Unfortunately there is going to be a risk of retaliation from an abuser no matter how serious the abuse is. Once you get involved with an abuser there is always the risk that he will want to get back at you, or try to reclaim you, or feel that if he "can't have you, nobody will"— I am afraid this is a reality you will have to live with as long as he is alive, or as long as he is not in a foreign country able to get back here. Some extreme abusers (especially in crime organizations or the underworld) will kill a victim by proxy, so perhaps even in this scenario you are never completely safe. Such abusers may even have a vendetta to kill you even if the abuser is already dead. It is going to be like living in a very bad neighborhood from now on, and you just have to muster up all the various means of protection you have until he no longer breathes. You will no longer live your life without risk.

As I will show in the next chapter, Nicole Simpson was never fully free from the risk of being harmed by her abuser OJ Simpson, even after she divorced him and moved away and clearly had moved on. He was a jealous and possessive fiend and killed Nicole out of jealousy and that mentality which says, "If I can't have her, nobody will." My birth mother was intimidated for years by her abuser over custody issues. My friend was harassed by her abuser when she tried to get the first of her protective orders by his threatening to harm her parents. My abuser made me fear that if I were to really leave, he would steal the children from me while I was asleep and disappear with them.

If you see and heed any of the warning signs I discussed in the previous chapter, you will see that if you remain, the risk for violence and even death increases, and if you get out early, the chances of violence and even death decreases. But if you get involved with an abuser, wittingly or not, you potentially face risks every day of your life, until he is dead. Fear of the unknown. If you get comfortable in your abusive situation, the fear of the unknown may seem terrifying compared to what you already know. *Will he try to come after me? Will he try to kill me? What he if goes nuts in a jealous rage? Will he go after my new boyfriend or lover? Is he going to follow me? Will I be able to sleep at night? Is he going to take the kids and run away? What if he finds me? What if I go back after I leave, what then? What will he do next? Will he destroy my property? Can I predict his behavior? Is he going to be worse? Is he going to back off? Is he going to take me seriously? What if he violates the protective order? What if I tell people, what are they going to say? What will people think of me? Can't he just leave me alone? What do I do next? How will the kids and I survive? How can I make him believe me that I never want to see him again? Will I ever be able to move on from this? What if he destroys my property and personal things if I go to the shelter? How can I get my stuff out safely? Who is going to believe me? How can I possibly get out of this? Do I have the strength to get away from him? What does the future hold for me?*

The fears and questions are legion. I often think that a disorder of thinking is either already present in the mind of the woman who is a potential abuse victim, or that the abuse engenders a disorder of thinking, or one feeds off of the other. Much of what I have written in Warning Signs of Abuse is in the form of a mental dialogue or thought processes— to illustrate the kinds of thoughts that occur to us before we get into abuse, as we get into abuse, what we think when we are in abuse, what we think when we get out of abuse, and what the abuser thinks when he is abusing you.

*Speak your thoughts.* Speak them to someone close to you, speak them to a counselor or minister, speak them in the form of journal writing. Are you thinking in any of the ways I am describing here? If you can detach your thoughts from yourself a bit, and then take a look at them, you might be able to analyze them and see if there is a disorder in any of them, or if the thinking process is not wholly rational or logical or based in fact. You may also find the roots of your abuse vulnerability. For instance, if I had verbalized the fact that I thought that being with an abuser was the best thing I was going to get in life, instead of just thinking it, perhaps someone in my social circle at the time could have helped me see that as a faulty thought. If I had written it down, maybe I could have looked at it and said, "Wow, I must really feel bad about myself." Then I could have worked on my low self-esteem and perhaps gotten out at that early point. If I had verbalized the fact that he was making me afraid early on— especially after he broke into my apartment that night while I was asleep— maybe someone would have then been able to tell me that this much fear is no basis for a loving relationship or marriage. Even later on, if I had written down my fears of the unknown— like finances, his threats, his reactions— I could have analyzed them and been able to answer them in a more concrete and logical fashion. Sometimes leaving thoughts to fester in your head can exacerbate their power over you, but speaking them out, or writing them out, can be an aid to diminishing their power over you and their effect on your behaviors and choices. It is also very cathartic to get something out that is really worrying you or bothering you. If you are sliding into abuse or are already in it is important to have a support group, counselor, prayer meeting, understanding friend or family member, or online forum, as well as a journal, to speak out your thoughts and then take a good look at them with a bit of detachment from yourself and feedback from others.

I wish I had done this much more than I did in the beginning especially, but I perhaps was afraid to burden my friends with all my inner machinations. I also was not completely honest with even my counselor about how bad things were, and because I did not speak out my thoughts there was no way to get a proper mirror of the situation, and see where the problems in my thinking were coming from. Some of the fears of the unknown are definitely justifiable: how will I survive this? what will he do in retaliation? These are not disordered fears under the circumstances. But living with the fears in your head and not trying to take steps towards a solution to them is going to keep you swirling around in anxiety and despair and hopelessness and inaction. Verbalizing the fears is a first step at trying to come up with real and practical solutions that can get you free from your abusive situation. If you can see what you are thinking you can take steps to change the thinking or change the circumstances that are causing the thinking.

*Threats.* It is very hard to change your circumstance if you are being told that doing so will bring about pain or injury or trouble. The problem is, you are already in trouble and in pain and are being injured. Can you take the gamble, can you make a plan to escape? Very difficult if he is threatening you. This is probably the most paralyzing thing an abuser can do to a woman to keep her in bondage and hinder any attempt she makes to be free.

*The "remorse" phase of the cycle keeps you in.* Your relationship is indeed like a series of perverse orgasms. Something stimulates, tension builds, an explosion occurs, there is a diffusion of energy, a waning, a purgation and a calm. And then it starts again. Yes, he hit you last night, but isn't he being so sweet today? He made you coffee. He kissed your cheek. He even bought your flowers. And didn't he pray with such contrition and such sincerity? This is the sweet guy you got attracted to in the first place, right? You want so much to believe that after that horrible event is always going to be like it is now. *He is trying so hard! He really is sorry, isn't he? Isn't it right to be forgiving? We all make mistakes. I am sure I we can work it through this time. It hasn't been that many times that he hurt me after all. God certainly wants me to be forgiving. If I can't give him a second chance, or another chance, what kind of Christian am I? We have our entire relationship or marriage at stake. Surely we can go on from here. He is like a new man now! Wow, I wish he were like this all the time!*

But he is not like this all the time, because something will come along again to incite his anger or control issues and he will lash out at you again, he will curse at you, he will put you down, he will threaten you, he will hit you, he will hurt you. It will cycle again and again. You have to see that the way he is acting in this phase of the cycle is not the way he acts all the time. Isn't that a warning sign if there ever was one? If he is only this way some of the time, then who is he really? The man you are seeing now is another mask or persona, like his affable superego that can charm a crowd or woo you and entrap you. But the real man is the one who has hurt you and damaged you and is damaging you now with these mixed behaviors. It will keep you in bondage and it is one of the threads that attached to your vulnerability, your religious beliefs, your emotional sensitivity, your heart.

It hurts me to this day that I forgave him over and over during these "contrition" phases. Like any woman, I wanted to be appreciated and cherished and protected and defended and adored and satisfied and loved. I guess it felt that way during some of those phases, but what I ultimately experienced during my entire twenty-four years with my abuser was degradation and destruction and pain and trauma. I am still recovering from the effects that his whirling and mercurial behaviors had on me.

For those of you who are Christian and who otherwise believe in forgiveness, the kind of forgiveness I am talking about here is not the forgiveness where you do not hold a person's sins against them. I am talking about returning again and again to the abuse and staying in the abuse because you forgave. I believe you can forgive your abuser in your heart and mind, but you do not have to live with him anymore, or even talk to him anymore. You do not have to wake up every day in this horrid life because you love God and want to do his will.

God's "will." I used to think I was doing his will by staying in my situation. I believed in second chances, or the hundredth chance. I believed that it would be shallow and lacking in faith not to give him another go. I eventually told my counselor this years later, but one of the things that did cause me to go back to the situation after I had determined to leave before we ever got married was my counselor saying to me, "Well, Theresa, don't give up on him yet." I had mustered all my resolve to finally get away, and she says this! I was so weak and already so damaged by the abuse that I was actually greatly influenced by what my counselor had said to go back to the situation instead of getting away.

In her defense, I am not sure I was completely honest about everything he had said and done to me by that point. She knew enough that when I told her we were getting married, she said she and her husband— who was like a father to me— would not attend. I was so desperate for them to attend that I came back some weeks later to tell them we had "worked out our problems" and everything was "fine" and there was no more abuse and he was all changed and delivered and healed and everything was great. It was at that point that they acquiesced to come to the wedding and that her husband walked me down the aisle.

But another warning sign was that one friend of mine refused to come to the wedding because she knew about the abuse. That was undoubtedly born of the same spirit of concern that I had for my close friend who was entering into a marriage that I felt was going to go abusive.

Whole religions and cults and government systems and ideologies are based on the domination and control of one group, sex or entity over another. I sought out and joined a particular religious community in the desperate belief that their particular way of submission of the woman to the man, wife to husband, was indeed the way and will of God. Everything else I had tried up to that point to bring change to my abuser failed. I earnestly tried to follow this particular way to the point of changing my dress and my appearance and being as "submissive" as I could figure out how to be. What I got in return was judgment from the community when I shared how horrible my situation was, because the fault obviously lay with me: I was just not being submissive enough. What I got in return from my abuser was more abuse. Towards the end I literally would pray for him to die.

I cannot see any relationship between two people that causes pain and trauma and injury and fear and unhappiness and misery and depression and destruction and degradation and woe and hurt and disgust and repulsion and anguish and ruin to be the will of God. Surely there is something cruelly amiss between what is the product of abuse and what should be the very fruit of love: happiness, joy, fulfillment, respect, appreciation, admiration, fervor, tenderness, consideration, health, safety, protection, satisfaction, comfort, laughter, rest and peace. In abuse you have all the evil, and the good you think is there is a shadow and a fleeting lie and bondage.

Never, ever believe that what you have suffered or you think you may suffer with an abusive man is the will of God, or morally right, or justifiable, or okay. It is definitely as big a problem as you think it is or as others think it is. Your sufferings are not small and unimportant and they did happen and they will continue to happen. You have to see that getting out at the earliest warning sign will be the healthiest and safest thing you can do for yourself and your future, and getting away at any point is worth the inherent risks involved.

## COPING AND MAINTAINING

I do understand that you may not think you need to get out just now. I understand that you feel you cannot get out ever. I understand that you straddle between thinking it is okay and wanting to leave. I understand that you may have left and gone back. I understand that there are reasons why you feel you need to stay. I understand that you think about it but are not sure what to do, or when, or how.

*Coping.* There is no judgment from me here. Let's assume that you are staying. You do see that there are problems and yes, he has hurt you, but you are staying because you think he will change and you are going for counseling and he is in anger management and you have kids. Maybe you just feel it would be too much right now. Maybe you are too afraid to do it right now. Maybe it would be nice to just get through each day a little easier.

*Getting through each day.* I often found that retreating to my own space when he got angry or insane was helpful. What I mean is going into my bed, or into my own mind and prayers.

*Minimize conflict.* I am serious that your responding back to him in kind will only incite him. You may be saying everything right, but it does not matter what you say. You need to not incite him. If he starts yelling, do not yell back. Do not try to make him see that he is wrong. You cannot ever do it so do not try. Do not try to justify yourself to him. Say nothing. Better this than getting into an argument that might lead to an altercation or violence. I am certainly all for equality of women and men, but in the case of abuse you cannot afford to try to equal him if he is yelling or getting violent. You ultimately are the stronger of the two of you. He is weak and that is why he tries to dominate you. A true man of true strength is not intimidated by the strength of any female, or by a female for any reason. So know this in yourself while he is going off. Remind yourself that you are strong, you are dealing with so much, and right now you are not going to feed the fire. Someday you will be free of the situation, but for now you are going to diffuse the situation and not cause him to become more violent or abusive to you. Remember that he is the coward and the loser, and you are the strong warrior!

*Capitulate.* This goes with minimizing conflict. So what if he is yelling and telling you that you are a horrible housekeeper and what a mess everything is? So what if he starts going nuts because you burnt to food on the stove? So what if he thinks you are fat and calls you some name? I found that the biblical adage to "agree with your adversary quickly" is useful in abuse situations where you need to keep the immediate situation from getting worse. And in the end, if you control your reactions, you get the upper hand. Do you want a fight? Do you want him to keep yelling? Do you want him to break more things? So you can say, "Yeah, I'm really sorry, things really are a mess today." Inside yourself you might be thinking *"You %&*$#, clean it up yourself if you don't like it"* — but do you see where that will take you? Then he will hit you, or break something, or keep yelling. I am talking about a survival skill here, not your attempt to justify yourself to him or the universe or make all things right. So you can say, "I am really sorry I burnt dinner. Would you like me to make something else now, or can it wait until tomorrow and I can try again?" Of course you want to tell him to f— off, but where will that get you? Into a fight and an argument. Of course he is wrong, but in these situations you cannot afford to be right! You can say, "Yep, I am fat all right. Gotta start working out." Of course you want to tell him that he is a degenerate son of a bitch, but then what? Do you want an argument that will get the police called? Do you want to make him hit you? You have to be your own best friend in these situations.

Think about what you are doing and why. I do recognize that sometimes we are subconsciously making the situation worse, because maybe if it gets really bad then maybe we really will try to get out, or maybe the police really will come and maybe this time he will really get arrested and this time he will go to jail or this time I will finally go get the protective order. Try to engage your mind and see if you can figure out why you might be making the situation worse. In a normal situation it would be right and acceptable for you to stand up for yourself and call out a wrong against yourself, but you are not in a normal situation. You are with a volatile, manipulative, potentially violent person whose first line of defense against his own weakness is hurting you. So realize that in these cases fighting back may get you injured or killed.

*Pamper yourself.* For me, it is a very hot tub with Lavender mineral salts and my favorite Indian Satya Sandalwood incense and maybe a few tea lights. Or it might be a new special pair of underwear. Or maybe a new book or kitchen item. You can do so much to make yourself feel better and it only needs to cost a couple of dollars, or nothing at all. I often would need these little devices to help put salve on the woundings from his words or his hand.

*Deep breathing.* As a voice teacher I advocate deep breathing for singing as well as for helping with stressful situations and for helping with self-control. One way to find a deep breath is to sit on a chair with your back forward, off the seat, with your elbows on your knees. Take a breath that feels like the beginning of a yawn, deep into yourself. You will find that you do not raise your shoulders when you breathe this way, which is a good thing. You will feel your breath expand down in your belly and around your ribs and even around your back. Try it with a relaxed jaw, slowly in, slowly out, beginning of a yawn feeling. After a few breaths deep like this, exhale slowly on a "hssssss." See how long you can make that "hssss" last, keeping the feeling of openness as if you are still breathing in. Eventually you can slowly and deeply breathe in and out as you get used to the sensations in your breath and body. The first few times you do this you might feel a little light-headed, but eventually you can find you can do a deep breath when you need to feel calmer or are anxious and it really helps. You can do deep breathing while you are standing or driving or sitting still or laying down. I have a link to a detailed article I wrote on deep breathing in the Sources and Resources section at the end of the book.

*Keep an online journal.* I do not recommend keeping a written journal in the house, because he will find it. If you can get out, go to the library and write there. What I often do is email materials I have written to myself. But if you know how to blog then you can keep an online blog, but I would keep it private by not mentioning any names and I would not publish it publicly. In this online journal you can keep record of specific incidents—if you are up to recording it. For instance: "July 1st, 2014. Slapped me on the back of my neck and now I feel like I have whiplash." "August 23 2014 told me he was going to throw me down the stairs because I was not feeling well and I asked him to get a drink of water for me." An online journal would be a great place to ventilate and think about your situation. It will give you a record and a way to look at the overall condition of your relationship and help you provide evidence you may need someday in a legal situation.

*Make phone calls.* These days with a cell phone you can reach a domestic violence hotline anywhere you are. In fact domestic violence shelters are now giving cell phones to all women who are at the shelter so they can have quick access to police services. You can call the hotline anonymously anytime, seven days a week. It is really good to talk to someone who will not judge you and who will listen to your tears and be able to help you either maintain or get out. I called many times over the years and I was glad I could talk when I needed to. Sometimes you really do not want to bother your friends or family and especially if something happens in the middle of the night it is good knowing that they are there. One word of caution: do not call the hotline when your abuser is there. You really have to learn to do things with stealth and care so as to get what you need in a volatile life situation.

Prepare a "flight bag." Have a bag ready with things you may need at a short notice, and one for your children as well. If you have to go to a shelter or take flight to your family or a friend or a hotel, at least you don't waste precious time in a precarious or dangerous situation.

## KEEPING RECORDS

You can do some things while you are waiting for the right time to leave or if you are planning to leave. Even though you are still in the situation, there is a sense of patient anticipation that someday you will get out and you kind of have this goal in mind as you bide your time.

*Keep records.* Use your online journal as a place to keep what you write. If you have any documents (such a threatening letter) it would be a good idea to make a copy of it and upload it to your cloud storage. Then give another copy to someone who you trust will keep it safe and not mention it to the abuser. You don't want it to look like a weird collection of events, but it would be good to record the date of an event and the injury if any. If you have ever had a witness to any scenario to which the police were not called and they are willing, get a written statement from them. Get copies of any police reports.

Part of the reason you need to do this is because your abuser will attempt to make it look like you are framing him, or doing what you are doing out of spite. If you go for a protective order you have to prove to the judge that you have a need for it, because usually the abuser is evicted from the home and this is a pretty serious thing for a man who likes his power and control.

*Take pictures.* This seems a bit macabre but I took pictures of most of my injuries. I actually had them in a photo album. Now I cannot find it and I think my abuser found it and destroyed it. If you have pictures of injuries it can provide proof of abuse, should you need to give testimony in court and did not have the police involved in the incident. It actually will help you gain a sense of reality over the sense of unreality that being injured by someone who says they love you does to you. If you can also remember or provide a date of injury this will be helpful down the road. You may think taking pictures of your injuries to be a bit bizarre, but as we will see in the next chapter, Nicole Simpson also took pictures of her injuries from OJ, and kept them in a safe deposit box. I have had to use a picture I took with my cell phone as proof of an injury to someone who did not believe my abuser would do such a thing to me.

*Research.* I spent a lot of time reading about abuse, learning about abusers, looking at online forums, finding out what support systems were in my area, what housing options were available to me, what my legal rights were, what my choices were.

## COUNSELING AND SUPPORT

Over the years I did have counselors and I did seek support from family and friends and my various church communities. It was very helpful to know I could always call the domestic violence hotline and talk about a recent incident or my desire and plans to get away. One of my dearest friends and closest confidant listened and encouraged me for years and still does, even now that I am free. I have been blessed with prayer and tears and hugs and gifts of money and food and clothing. I am grateful for these rays of light during years when it was very dark and I was in the dark night of the soul.

My only criticism is that some people and even some ministries do not know how to handle abusive situations very well. It seems sometimes like putting a band-aid on an open wound. It was very sweet when I was given bags of food or they helped pay the electric bill or helped fix my car. But what I needed was a place I could have lived rent-free while I rested and healed from the trauma I had been through for so long and then begin to rebuild my life and my ability to earn a living and support my children. A family member came pretty close to setting this up for me at one point but it never materialized. A minister offered me a place in another state but the situation was not right for my young children and me. I had attempted to tell my wealthy adoptive mother about the scenario but we became estranged before the visit was even over. There was a shelter and longer-term housing scenario about twenty-five miles away from me in a degenerated neighborhood and this would have entailed pulling my children out of the rural private school where they were on scholarship, and their friends and their church. So I was often between a rock and hard place in terms of my options and decisions. But I am glad for the support I did receive and I know it helped me get through until I got free.

You cannot manage dealing with abuse on your own. If you have not told anybody then you need to tell someone. Even if you think it is a small issue, tell someone about it. It is very good to get feedback, because maybe it is indeed worse than you think it is. Maybe by talking to someone you will find a place to stay or a ministry or organization that can help you or someone to help you move. Some areas not only have a domestic violence shelter, but also offer support groups in addition to legal services for abuse victims. I never liked group therapy much but, looking back, it might have done me good to go. If you can manage it then try as many options as you can. I know you can feel hopeless and degraded and afraid and embarrassed but tell someone somehow— a private counselor or minister, a support or prayer group, a friend or family member, or a domestic violence hotline. The next chapter is a case study of Nicole Brown Simpson and OJ Simpson. Nicole lived in abusive marriage with OJ Simpson for years, bore him two children, finally got away, and was ultimately murdered by him. Her life story is a life lesson of abuse.

# CHAPTER SIX: NICOLE BROWN SIMPSON (1959-1994) AND OJ SIMPSON

*"I'm afraid this man will kill me someday."* — Nicole Brown Simpson

*"O.J did it! O.J killed her! I knew that son of a bitch was going to kill her!"* — Denise Brown, sister of Nicole Brown Simpson

*"Nicole was a victim of domestic violence, abused and battered by the man she loved during their life together and despite his repeated declarations of love and his regret at having hurt her in the past, I also believe that on Sunday, June 12, 1994, he murdered her."* — Tee Bylo

A whole book could be written on the subject of Nicole Brown Simpson and OJ Simpson, and indeed, many books have been written— from scores of books on the OJ Simpson trial, to books about the life of Nicole Brown Simpson, and covering topics from spousal abuse and domestic violence to race relations to police corruption, to the travesty and farce that was his trial and acquittal.

I was fascinated as was most of America the day the infamous white Ford Bronco was being shown driving in a low-speed chase over in California with some old football player guy trying to run from a murder charge. Suddenly this became headline news and remained headline news and anytime OJ Simpson has done anything since it has been headline news.

My adoptive mother died in early 1995 during the OJ Simpson trial and I used it as a form of what I call "RAT" therapy, or "Reality Avoidance Therapy" in order to cope with my grief. I watched the trial from start to finish, and my mouth hung open in utter disbelief when not only was OJ

Simpson acquitted, but a great number of Americans cheered. Since then I have read many books on the trial and on Nicole Brown Simpson and have developed my own perspective on her marriage and relationship with OJ Simpson and why he murdered her and how he got away with it.

Nicole Brown Simpson and her friend Ron Goldman were found dead in the walkway of Nicole's Brentwood, California condo on June 6th, 1994. Nicole's throat was slashed from ear to ear and her head was nearly cut off. Ron Goldman was stabbed in the neck and face and side as if grabbed from behind or the side and repeatedly slashed and punctured. Her ex-husband OJ Simpson was soon after charged with murder and eventually brought to trial which was televised and covered for many months. OJ Simpson was ultimately acquitted of murdering two people but is currently in jail in Nevada serving a sentence for an unrelated robbery offense. He was also eventually found responsible for the deaths of Nicole Brown Simpson and Ron Goldman in a civil wrongful death trial and has been ordered to pay punitive and compensatory damages to the Brown and Goldman families.

I identified with Nicole Brown Simpson and I still do. She was only three years older than I am. She had a strong personality as I have and was outspoken towards her abuser, as I was. After her divorce she dropped her married name as I did when I got my divorce. She had children with her abuser as I did, and had them well after the abuse had started, as I did. She stayed in her abusive relationship for a very long time, as I did. She took pictures of her injuries as I did. She tried to get away from her abuser as I did. She tried to move on with her life, as I have so far. But that is where the similarities end, because she is dead and I am still here.

I suppose I was also living the OJ trial vicariously, as if it were my abuser on trial and the world would see who he really was and what he did to me and I would finally be vindicated. The travesty that was trial and acquittal of OJ Simpson left a deep sense of indignation in me and against my abuser and is an open wound that is with me to this day.

One good thing that came out of the OJ Simpson trial was a raising of the national awareness about the realities of spousal abuse and domestic violence. What grieves me is that the whole case became more about cops and race than it was about two people dying a horrible and unjustifiable death, and the fact that the woman had been the victim of repeated severe domestic violence. If the murderer and the victims had been of the same race, he would have never been acquitted and the issue of domestic violence would have been what the whole case was about. It was a travesty of justice on so many levels. What should have been an object lesson by way of a media celebrity became a cause célèbre for a media celebrity.

## THE VOICE OF NICOLE BROWN SIMPSON

*"OJ: After all these years together, there are still some things that we have to get straight. One is that you think I want control of you, which is totally wrong - I only want of you, what you, so easily and strongly expect of me. Secondly, Don't ever tell me that I want everything for myself - that I want a million dollar house etc. - that's total bologna! Because I didn't start that conversation in the first place. And when you get mad at me, like, trying to stop you from doing too much cocaine, and you get mad— you're wrong! And you have no right to get upset. And you know*

*down inside that that is what I so strongly object to— especially when you are spending three hours trying to avoid it— I rest my case. I am not wrong trying to pull you out of there— and if you wouldn't have found more coke (cocaine), you wouldn't have been there this long. I don't want to marry you. And I don't want a family by you...so let's just leave you and I as we are - you have cheated on me - and I'll never doubt that - and that's something about you that probably won't change - So let's accept life as it is - I've asked you to work on the coke - you don't! That's all - No hard feelings on my part - I've tried. I just think that I try a little harder than you."*—Nicole Brown Simpson, before her marriage to OJ Simpson in 1985

In analyzing this letter I can see an intelligent, strong and articulate woman who shows great courage and strength in dealing with a relationship involving drugs, infidelity, and abuse. She is clearly crying out that she is not loved or appreciated: being yelled at, cheated on, accused falsely, not given credit for caring, being undervalued and devalued. All the signs of an abusive relationship are there— she has been with him up to seven years by this point:

*Deflection:* OJ is accusing her of being controlling, when he is the one who is controlling her

*False accusations:* accusing Nicole of being materialistic and unloving, when she clearly cares for him and not his money. He is the one who is not caring for her and is cheating on her

*Hitting her weak spots:* attacking the value of her love and feeling for him and her actions in trying to help him

*A window into the abuse:* she talks about him getting "angry," "mad" and "upset" over her trying to care for him— responses which are not normal in normal people

*A sense of resignation:* she already tells him "no hard feelings" when she has every right to have hard feelings. She clearly feels violated and hurt and unhappy. The abuse has already begun to wear her sense of resolve. There is an undercurrent of feeling unloved and unappreciated but she is already resigned to what she sees is her fate

*A sense of indignation:* She clearly wants to make things right in the relationship and wants OJ to see his wrongs in the relationship. "I am not wrong;" "You have no right to be upset;" "I want from you what you expect of me." I give her a lot of credit for speaking as strongly and courageously as she did at this point, when abuse was clearly under way and its hold was clearly upon her. It is up to her to make it right: She is taking on the responsibility of trying to help OJ with his drug problem, when for every drug abuser the responsibility for change is with himself. She is already feeling that the problem is with her own inability to make it right and not with the drug abuser's inability to make it right.

I wish Nicole has gotten out at this point, before she married OJ and had children with him. At this point she writes that she did not even want to be married or have children with him. Perhaps she somehow sensed how horrible things would become if she did get married and have children with him. It is possible that she already felt the fear of setting him off and was just content to keep riding the waves of abuse as they were. If I knew what I know now and could have talked to her, I would have begged her with all my being to get out of the relationship right then and there, I would have given her a place to stay if she needed it, and I would have been there for her through each step of the way until she was free. But is possible that somehow deep within her, she knew she would never be free, and that even with a divorce and a new life he was going to continue to abuse her with all his strength and vengeance until he took away her very last breath.

## WHAT HAPPENED IN THE LIFE OF NICOLE BROWN SIMPSON, AND WHY WAS SHE MURDERED BY OJ SIMPSON?

*He picked her.* Like every predator he sought his prey. Nicole was only seventeen years old and just out of high school and working as a waitress when she met OJ. She was very beautiful, tall, blonde, gorgeous figure, and OJ saw the potential in her. She was flattered and smitten by the attentions of this rich and famous football hero. But he was not just attracted to her because of her beauty. There was vulnerability in her. She was young and in some ways less experienced and he no doubt saw her malleability. He could make her into the trophy wife he had yearned to have. He was also married when he and Nicole began their relationship and it has been reported that OJ was glad to find a woman whom he could hang on his arm— a white woman, a living Barbie doll. OJ wanted to join and be accepted in the social world of Hollywood and for him, having a white wife was the means for him to do it.

*He groomed her.* He flattered her and he showered her with attention. He had money and he bought her expensive things and took her on expensive trips. She entered the world of the rich and famous as a teenager just out of high school. Even Nicole later admitted that she had been "clay" and OJ "sculpted" her into the trophy wife he desired. She said that OJ literally "changed her personality to reflect the idea of the perfect woman" and that she was "his creation." He subjugated her naturally attractive and congenial personality and she learned how to temper herself when it was necessary to survive. But I do see a resiliency in her, that she did assert herself with her abuser and showed great strength even though he had ruined her thinking processes and her ability to make sound choices. And in her case, it seems she genuinely loved him, and wanted the relationship to work, even though he abused her for seventeen years and she endured many beatings and repeated threats against her life.

*He controlled her.*

*"That O.J. Simpson guy brought me a lot of pain and heartache - I tried so hard with him - I wanted so to be a good wife. But he never gave me a chance. "*—Nicole Brown Simpson

*"Make no mistake. Nicole knew OJ was dangerous— we all did. And I truly believe that she realized his violence could end in murder. "*— Faye Resnick

OJ established very hard and fast boundaries for her and became fiercely jealous and possessive if any one looked at her or she danced in public and got noticed. Yet he cheated on her with abandon as if it was his privilege. He became insanely furious and would start cursing at her if she even mentioned the name of another man in his presence. He was a wild man and an ogre and a hugely physically strong man who could have killed anyone with the pinch of his fingers. He had an irrational and explosive temper and got so angry he would heave and sweat with rage. Like every abuser, he sought to gain power and control in life through power and control over his victim. He very much sucked the life out of Nicole and lived through sucking her energy from her. To me he is one of the most disgusting human beings on the planet— and tigers and lions who trap and eat their prey alive should look up to him as an example of how to do it.

Even Nicole suspected his desire to control her was to be her demise. Unless you are dying of a terminal disease, it is very unusual for a 35-year old woman to write a last will and testament— but Nicole did just that, a mere five weeks before her murder. This will, and the photographs of her injuries, were found in her safe deposit box after her murder— saved, in a sense, for posterity, for the media, for her ultimate vindication. Some people do have a premonition or sense that they are going to die— and Nicole no doubt was trying in some way to "put her house in order" before her premature death, and perhaps leave her tragic legacy as an example for the world to see.

*He killed her.*

*"OJ is using a knife to settle a score."*— Christopher Darden, Attorney for the Prosecution *"OJ wanted to control Nicole and failed. And in failing, found the one way where he could keep her under control where she could never slip out of it again."*—Marcia Clark, Attorney for the Prosecution

My understanding of the murder scenario was that OJ was at the scene of the crime already stalking Nicole, but he was also dressed for an attack— in dark clothes, with a dark knit ski cap, wearing leather gloves, but oddly enough, wearing expensive and uncommon, high-end Bruno Mali shoes. (These were the shoes that he called "ugly-ass" during the trial but had been photographed wearing before. The defense claimed the photos of him wearing the shoes had been photoshopped, and even through bloody shoe prints from the crime scene matched those shoes and his large shoe size.) Her friend Ron Goldman happened to come to the door of her South Bundy Drive condo to deliver some eyeglasses that her mother had left at the restaurant where they had all dined earlier that evening, which was ironically named "The Mezzaluna,"— a type of long knife. Poor Ron Goldman was in the wrong place at the wrong time. It has been established that he and Nicole were not lovers (which is significant in that OJ may have perceived them to be) and that he simply came by to return the glasses. But it also seems OJ saw this man with his victim and his jealous and possessive anger drove him to kill them both. It could have been that he killed Goldman first and then when Nicole came to the door her killed her. Another theory is that he came there with the intent of killing her. When he was finishing with killing Nicole, Goldman unexpectedly appeared, and he killed him in his bloody fury to silence a witness.

*He got away with it.*

*"I also believe that OJ will not be convicted of murder, primarily because of racial tensions in Los Angeles and because the legal system has no rational, modern system for selecting a jury able to cope with the social pressures and legal complexities of the trial."*—Jon Katz, Wired Magazine 1995

The preponderance of evidence against OJ— from blood evidence everywhere, from the walkway where the murders occurred to his car to his house and even his socks— not to mention copious DNA evidence, shoe prints, and his erratic behavior following the murders— would have been enough under normal circumstances to convict any man a hundred times over. But these were not normal circumstances. There were serious faults in jury selection, trial venue, the defense team arguments, media coverage and political opportunism by certain community leaders, as well as an incompetent judge who seemed more interested in getting his face in the news than administering justice in a courtroom. It is clear to me that had race not played such a devastating role in the OJ Simpson trial, he would have been convicted after a five-minute deliberation by even a jury of below average intelligence or a panel of twelve children.

Over and over again OJ was able to use his charming persona and status as a star athlete and media personality to beguile the police who were called so many times to intervene in domestic violence incidences over the years. Nicole even complained that they "never did anything" to OJ no matter how many times they were called to her home or how visible were her injuries. It seems even the police were under the spell of this man. Some of them used to even play basketball in OJ's private Brentwood court in their off-duty hours. Police and detectives spoke endearingly of the "great football player" and this even seemed to cloud how they questioned him after the murders and how seriously they looked at evidence in the beginning. And there is no doubt in my mind that a severe disorder of thinking caused a whole subculture in America to fail in coming to a logical and dispassionate conclusion about the verdict. This was no place for race and race should have never, ever played a part in the OJ Simpson trial. It was a travesty of justice that the race card was allowed and even encouraged in the trial and in the media, and a worse travesty that so many people believed its role regarding evidence in the trial and continue to believe it to this day.

I give Nicole so much credit and I admire this beautiful and strong woman for all she endured and how much she accomplished in trying to get free. In cases of maniacs like OJ I am not sure a woman can ever live free from worry of an attack like this. It seems that at the time of her murder things were on somewhat of an even keel with

OJ and in my knowledge of the case she never got a protective order against him. She did know he could kill her, and had threatened to kill her, and she even said that he was going to someday kill her. Perhaps she felt that because he was by that point in a relationship with someone else that he had given up and was going to leave her alone. I know in my own case I worry that someday my abuser is going to come after me and that he may even go after a former lover of mine if he ever finds out about it. I still worry about the ex-husband of my friend that I helped get free. He is also a true maniac and very jealous and possessive and I could see him trying to find her and kill both her and her new husband.

## THE AFTERMATH AND LEGACY OF THE OJ SIMPSON VERDICT

*"The money is not the issue. It never has been. It's holding the man who killed my son and Nicole responsible."*—Fred Goldman, father of Ron Goldman

The perversity of justice which was the OJ Simpson murder trial did not stop the tenacious Fred Goldman and the Brown families from seeking justice for Ron and Nicole. There were also many Americans who shared the sense of a travesty that unfolded before their eyes, and calling OJ Simpson into account in civil proceedings seemed to all like the natural and just progression of events in a sad and traumatic series of events. In 1997 the Brown and Goldman families won their wrongful death civil lawsuit against OJ Simpson for the deaths of Nicole Brown Simpson and Ronald Goldman. OJ was ordered to pay $25 million in punitive damages to both families and another $5 million in compensatory damages to the Goldman family, for a total of

$31.5 million. To this date the families have only been able to collect small portions of what is due them. What victories have come are largely due to the indefatigable Fred Goldman. Ron's father has been particularly persistent and resolute in his attempts at bringing OJ to accountability and obtain some kind of justice for his son Ron and for Nicole. One notable victory was the winning of rights to OJ's confessional book and the Goldman family being able to make money off the words of the man who killed their son. Another was forcing the sale of OJ's Heisman Trophy, which did yield a considerable sum, but nothing near what they were awarded or ever hope to collect.

It has been reported, not surprisingly, that OJ has been hiding his wealth in offshore accounts and moved to Florida years ago in an effort to avoid having his residence seized in civil judgment. It has astonished me that OJ has been able to evade justice over and over again and for so long. I have no doubt that Fred Goldman will pursue justice for Ron and Nicole and Nicole's children until the end of his life and even beyond, even if it is to keep OJ uncomfortable and irritated.

The state of race relations in the country seems worse today than it was when I was a child growing up in New York City in the '60's and '70's. I have often wondered at the extreme disparity of thinking and reactions to the OJ Simpson verdict between certain groups of whites and blacks and have wondered if the trial itself did not help cause even more damage and fracturing of the American psyche than what existed at the time due to the incendiary nature of the race card played by the defense. Then again, I have wondered if things were just bad anyway, and the trial was simply a mirror of the state of race relations as they then were. It could well be a combination of both. But people of all persuasions should know that women of all races and countries and cultures and societies and subcultures and ethnicities are victims of abuse, and that it is never a good thing to let an abuser and especially an abuser-murder escape justice. Mark Furhman may have been a racist, but OJ Simpson murdered Nicole Brown Simpson and Ron Goldman. I wish this had been the heart of the trial and nothing else.

Perhaps someday the trial will be looked back on with a sound mind of reason and not be tainted by emotion or historical racial antipathies and seen it for what it was: a woman (and innocent bystander) killed by her abuser. For the sake of abused women everywhere, I pray that this will be the legacy of the murders of Nicole Brown Simpson and Ron Goldman.

It is my hope that the murder of Nicole Brown Simpson would not be in vain. It is my hope that her slaughter, and the slaughter of her innocent bystander friend Ron Goldman, would be used for good, to educate about abuse and domestic violence and the perils of the abusive personality that found a particularly puerile embodiment in OJ Simpson. And it is my hope that, even if he is in jail for a different crime at present, he never sees the light of day again, and that the Brown and Goldman families get the financial and historical vindication that they have long sought on behalf of Nicole and Ron. I also hope that what happened to Nicole has been and continues to be used for good to help abused women in their own monumental struggles to be free. And I hope Nicole knows that I would have been her friend and that I would have understood.

# CHAPTER SEVEN: CONTROL YOURSELF: A PARADIGM SHIFT IN THE TREATMENT OF ABUSERS

## AGAINST POSITIVE AFFIRMATION

I do not think that "positive affirmation" or "self-esteem" building techniques work with abusive men. At minimum they are narcissists to begin with and so they already feel wonderfully full of themselves. If they are also sociopaths they already see the world through the lens of their own selves only, and if they are psychopaths they lack all normal human empathy and perhaps even empathy for themselves. To tell them how much their "precious whittle selves" are valued instills an even greater sense of self-importance than they already have and certainly do not need.

## NOT AVOIDING PAIN AND SUFFERING

Like drug addicts and alcoholics, abusers (who may also be drug addicts and alcoholics and usually are) choose to avoid certain painful feelings and act in ways to avoid feeling certain pain. A drug addict who is addicted to a drug like heroin is scared of the pain he will feel if he does not take the drug. An alcoholic is scared of the feelings he will feel if he does not drink. An abuser is scared of losing what control he thinks he has of the external world and thus takes his anger out on his female victim as a means of trying to reestablish or maintain what he thinks is his sense of control of the external world. Cowards all, feckless cowards all.

What feckless cowards need is a good hard dose of the pain they are avoiding. The drug addict needs to go through the pain of his withdrawal in order to be free. The alcoholic needs to cry and suffer and accept harsh realities as part of the process of this life so he will no longer try to drown them away. The abuser needs to learn how to control himself and not attempt to control the outside world or the females within it.

## CONTROL YOURSELF, NOT OTHERS

It would be a good thing if men who are narcissistic anyway could concentrate on something self-centered like self-control. They could learn, for instance, that refraining from yelling— learning to control the impulse to yell— will help them ultimately not get in trouble in social or personal situations or with the law. You could extend this to acts of violence such as throwing things and breaking things or more serious crime. They could learn that self-control feels good in some way and that it serves a higher purpose. The higher purpose for a narcissist is, of course, serving himself, so if the paradigm could shift to give the sense of power that bully-narcissist-abusers lack via self-control, perhaps women would cease to be less the target of rage and fury. They could then get angry at themselves for not fulfilling the desire for control and at not the outside world, which includes the women they abuse within it. This might work to a point.

Then of course is the concept that there are things which we can never control or ought to try to control. Because the bully-narcissist-abuser feels a loss of power and control, he feels the urge to find it through dominating someone weaker and more vulnerable than he is. The abuser needs to discover as the rest of the world has that no matter how hard you try, certain things are beyond our control and giving up control is part of life's lessons. This they cannot accept and they go berserk and hurt and kill because of the sense of loss of control at both the external and internal world. But unless the benefit outweighs the consequence no narcissist or sociopath or psychopath will ever endeavor to change. Some theories of the brain suggest they cannot, because they are wired differently and their brains lack normal empathic centers. Part of what I am suggesting finds its parallels in some anger management therapies, but will work better if it appeals to the self-centered nature of the abuser or angry person and not because he will see behavioral change as a benefit to anyone else. So the best is to encourage the one thing that every person is able to more or less control or can endeavor or learn to control: himself. They might gain just enough sense of control that they won't see it by dominating a woman. They will still be narcissists and sociopaths and psychopaths, and I do not recommend any woman getting into a relationship with a narcissist or a sociopath or psychopath but at least they might not hurt and kill women. Maybe I am dreaming but the reality is worse.

# CHAPTER EIGHT: I CLIMBED UP AND AWAY— AND YOU CAN, TOO

## SEVEN TIME'S THE CHARM

When I went to get my second-to-last protective order against my abuser, I apologized to the lawyer who was representing me for having gotten so many PFAs and rescinding them, over and over again. She told me that on average it takes a woman seven attempts to finally get free from an abusive relationship. In the end, it really was seven times before I was finally free.

The attempts to get out may take different forms. It may be a simple "sorry, but this relationship is not working out and I do not want to see you again" to getting a protective order to sneaking a move when he is at work to moving on with someone else. But each time you try to get away in some way is still an attempt get away.

Do not condemn yourself if you are still with him, or that you went back to him, or that you think about going back to him, or that you didn't even try to get away.

## WHY DO WE GO BACK?

The reasons why we go back are much the same reasons as why we stay. I have covered the reasons why we stay extensively in Chapter Five. Perhaps now we can look at them from the perspective of a woman who already has left at least once— you broke up, you left, you went to a shelter, you got an order and rescinded it.

*I am "committed" to making it work.* Sometimes you think you have lost some kind of moral integrity by actually leaving the relationship, especially if you are already married.

*My religion says I am supposed to go back.* Someone within your religious sphere has told you that you are really not obeying God if you fail to be a wife to your husband. Or this is the way you read the Bible or some religious work or what you heard in a sermon.

*My children miss their dad.* It is very true that they will miss their father if they had a close relationship with him in spite of the abuse. What I worried about was that they blamed me for tearing up the home, but it was his actions and not mine that cause me to do it. Yet a child cannot reason about it the way we wish and they will often simply blame you for "taking away" their dad. Realize also that eventually a visitation schedule can be made and that the kids will see him, if he is actually interested and committed to them, rather than to trying to manipulate you.

*I got pregnant.* But you do not have to marry an abuser because he got your pregnant. You do not have to stay with an abuser because he got you pregnant. You can move on and someday perhaps a better man will be a father to your unborn child. I understand the difficulties of getting pregnant in an abusive relationship— I was making concerted efforts to leave when I got pregnant the last three times. Each of my children remains the blessing and light of my life, but each has suffered greatly from having the father they have had. Maybe someday I will have a person in my life who can act in a non-abusive way and this can be healing to them.

*I am not sure I can make it without him.* This may be in part because he is making it difficult for you to be without him. Is he withholding money from you? Is he manipulating you about the kids? Is going to court for child support too much for you to deal with? Money is a primary factor in many women staying in abusive relationships. This segues into the next reason why we go back.

*Finances.* I needed his money if we did separate or divorce, but I did not want to go through the child support process, because he threatened to disappear and not support the kids if I took him to court. I believed him. I should have called his bluff and ridden the tide of uncertainty just a little while and it would have worked out. This one really kept me in bondage.

I honestly wish I had been more assertive with my adoptive mother, who was wealthy, when she was alive, before she disinherited me, and explained more clearly how bad the situation was to her. I never made it entirely clear and our "mother-daughter" relationship was always fractured and tenuous. But I should have done it anyway. As it is I got nothing from her and if I had been more honest maybe I would have, and would have gotten away long ago. But since her love towards me was decidedly "conditional" I am not sure if any of my real concerns or hurts ever mattered to her, or would have had I brought them to her. But this is not to discourage you from trying to get help from whatever family you do have.

I also should have been more assertive with my abuser's family. I guess part of me thought that they must see how bad it is, and if they had wanted to help they would have helped. I got close to getting serious support at one point but it never materialized. I guess I felt like I was not worth the trouble if they did not follow through with their offer. I also did not push it, but looking back I really should have pushed it. It is possible I could have been out many years before I finally did get out if I had simply pushed a little harder for financial help from both sides of the family and explained the depth of the problem more clearly.

I also did try to get help from various church groups and ministries, but what I really needed was a place to live rent-free with my kids for a while until I could get on my feet. This level of assistance never materialized. I did receive gifts of money, food, clothing, car repairs, a car, bill payments, rent forgiveness and even moving assistance, but it was always the fear of losing my home or something happening to the kids that kept me going back to the situation over and over again. In reality he never did give a great deal of money to us, and he was incredibly unreliable and irresponsible. He truly was and is a man who never deserved to have the wife and family he was given.

*You are already conditioned.* Being away feels awkward and you somehow feel you might have made a mistake. You lose resolve. It took so much effort to do all of it that you take what seems the easier road. It may be for the short run but in the end it is far more difficult. Your options did not work out. When I was at the shelter they had promised me a place for abused women where I could live rent free or reduced but it never materialized, so I went back to the home with him that I had left.

*Desperation.* He was never responsible or reliable but even what little he did give (in addition to what I was doing) kept us going. I had lost my inheritance and had no assistance from anyone, so it was better than nothing. I was scared to lose our home or have to leave the school district that my children were part of.

*You believe his lies.* He isn't going to do drugs anymore, cheat anymore, hit you anymore, it will be a fresh start. You want so much to believe it.

*His mercurial behavior.* He begins to act penitent and then you think it might work. But somehow you put how he acted last week out of your mind.

*In denial.* You tried to make it look better to others than it really was. You want to believe that everything is going to be okay, and you tell people that is it going to be okay, but deep inside do you believe it is going to be okay?

*Fear of the unknown.* Even though what you have lived through is horrible, the fear of the unknown may be worse.


KEYS TO BREAKING FREE

Write and talk your fears. I believe the main problem for the abused woman is the state of her mind and thought processes. If you are thinking in a disordered way then you will make disordered choices and these choices will end up hurting you in the end. What are you afraid of? Why don't you try to leave? What is holding you back? If you can write out your fears you can look at them more rationally and see if they are as bad as you think they are, or, if they are valid and concrete, actual ways to solve the problems that are scaring you. If you write them down then you have a record of the situation and a basis to discuss the fears with a pastor or counselor or friend or relative. By yourself or with the help of someone, you will be in a better position to see what is true and what is false, what is exaggerated and what is reasonable, what is irrational and what is rational, what is perverse and what is normal. Then you can discard the false fears and deal practically with the real fears.

*Accept that the situation is broken.* It is better to face the truth than perpetuate a lie and a fantasy. It really is this bad because you want to get out of it. It is pathological and unhealthy and perverse and abnormal. Even if you hold some hope that it will someday be better you cannot afford to stay in it now. If you accept it for what it is you can stop pretending to everyone around you that it is better than you know it really is. Denial will lead you deeper and deeper into the vortex of abuse in all its entrapments and entanglements.

*Tell people what is going on.* Sometimes this needs to be very concrete: "He knocked me on the floor today after a bad fight." "He called me a fucking bitch last night." "He told me I could not wear those shoes that I like for the party." "He threw the dinner dishes against the wall because I burnt the vegetables on the stove." Whatever it is, if you tell someone in plain and concrete terms then even if you do not believe it is as bad as it is someone else can tell you it is. You can get the necessary feedback to validate your choice to leave the relationship or attempt to get away. It is very important that you do not hide anything or stay silent. This keeps women entrapped because so much abuse is well-hidden and unless you talk about it no one will necessarily know. Keeping things hidden is one of the abuser's tricks. As you think about getting out, keep talking, keep sharing, keep getting validation and keep speaking the truth our so when you hear it you will know you are making the right choice.

*Keep records.* I have mentioned this in Chapter Five, but again, a paper trail is a very powerful tool in your survival and freedom arsenal. Pictures of injuries say everything. An account of a horrid fight or a threat made to you has great impact when written down. Copies of police reports will show the repeat nature of the offenses and establish for the outside world and for your own mind the seriousness of the situation.

*Stay socially connected.* Sometimes you do not want to talk about it and when you are in denial you see no reason to talk about it. But if you are trying to be free then it is very healthy and affirming and empowering to get involved in some sort of social validation— whether via traditional counseling, use of domestic violence hotlines, or a support group. Support groups are simply artificial social constructs centered around a particular social problem or medical condition. But since the social interaction is highly focused on a need, it can be a relief to find commonality with some of the people in your area that may be struggling with similar situations to your own.

*Research your options.* What do you know about the domestic violence shelter in your area? Do you know the crisis hotline number? Is there a support group in your neighborhood? Do you know how to get a protective order in your county or city? Is there supportive housing for women coming out of abuse? Have you looked at any domestic violence websites or online forums? Will your church help you? Have you asked family for support? Have you asked for financial help? Educate yourself, read, write, ask questions, collect information. But do not keep any brochures or flyers or printouts from web pages where your abuser can find them. Best to keep them with someone you can trust or in a place where he cannot find your educational materials.

*Ask for help.* You need to be bolder about this than you think. You need to be assertive here, especially if you have children involved. I know you feel debilitated and like you do not really matter anyway, but try to step outside yourself for a minute and see the woman crying in her bed, the woman in pain, the woman afraid, the tears and the bruises. That is you. Be your own best friend here, do it for that vision you just saw, even if it feels wooden and mechanical to do it.

*You also have to give up control: accept a period of uncertainty.* The familiarity of abuse may seem less intimidating than the specter of the unknown. The future is a phantom after all, and now is here! I can touch now and smell it and see it but down the road is a vapor and a mist. Yes, but every future was built on a present and every past was once a future. Every great decision ever made was made with an element of risk and uncertainty to it. If you can accept that you may not be able to control every aspect of what is coming down the road, then you can let go and let it come to you. You also have to give up control, even if it is the control of the present and the fear of the future. You can and should jump into the unknown, and the unknown will be more knowable the more you prepare and investigate and ask questions and listen to the testimony and counsel of others.

What if it all falls apart? I was afraid worst of all of losing whatever home we were in if I were to get away from him. In the end we did lose our home and I was still with him. You may indeed lose your home. You may need to go to a shelter, either a domestic violence shelter or a homeless shelter. You may have to go live with a friend or family or even a hotel room. I am sure options would have opened up to me if I had taken that plunge the last time, after I got divorced, instead of returning to the situation. Yet I was so depleted and unwell that I barely had the resolve to live at all. I hope you never let it get that bad.

Remember that whatever happens it is going to be temporary. The shelter visit will only be a few weeks. The stay at your friend's will only be for a few months. Eventually you will get food stamps if you need them. You will find housing, either public or private or through an agency. Eventually you will get some kind of support— either child support or welfare or disability. It grieves me that because I became too ill to function both mentally and physically that I eventually qualified for disability benefits, but now that money pays my rent each month. And I am well enough to work per diem part time as I feel I can and at this point have begun singing, writing and teaching again. My biggest fear was not writing out my fear and talking about it and seeing where the illogic was in it. If I had done that I think I could have made it work without him even years before I became disabled. I urge you to analyze your fears on paper, and then see what is real and what is perhaps illogical fear and what is doable and what cannot be done right now. This will empower you and give you a sense of control that you need yourself during this time of transition.

## THE FEARS AND REALITIES OF A PROTECTIVE ORDER

*Please note: I am addressing broad issues related to abuse and domestic violence in the American justice system, and not that of other countries. If you live in another country you will need to do research and make contacts to see what options are available to you.*

*Should you get a protective order?*

If it is getting so bad that you are thinking about getting protective order, you probably have needed to get one for some time. Has he ever hit you? Raised his hand or fist at you? Thrown you into anything? Thrown anything at you? Stalked you? Spied on you? Threatened you in any way? Pulled out a gun or waved a knife or rope at you? If you have broken up, is he still calling your or texting you or emailing you? Did you have to delete him from your social networking account? Has he made you feel frightened in any way by words or actions? Does he keep coming back at you even though you have begged him to stay away? Is he bothering any of your friends or family? Does he show up at church or the bar where he knows you hang out? Do you get some kind of "creepy feeling" about him? If you mentioned the need for a separation, did he go berserk? Did he threatened to sue you for custody of the kids if you mentioned divorce? Do you get the feeling he is following you? Has he broken into your home? Has he disabled your car or taken the keys so you cannot drive? Does he make you cry? Have you thought about getting an order, but are not sure how it is going to affect your life?

*When The Police Get Involved*

Sometimes the immediacy of the situation brings you into the world of the protective order whether you asked for it or not. States differ in their treatment of domestic violence situations, but in my state if the police are called or you call them, they are required to arrest the abuser if he has caused you a visible injury. This is an effort to keep the abuser from blaming the victim for his being arrested. Much as they would like to avoid admitting it, it does not always work. The times my abuser was arrested I was blamed by him anyhow, not really because the police were obligated to arrest him (although of course that pissed him off), but because I made the call in the first place. Then he would tell the police that I egged him into being hit or that he was defending himself against me, or that he really didn't mean to do it.

Whenever there is a domestic incident where there is a concern for your safety, the police will advise you as to your legal rights to an order of protection, whether or not the abuser is arrested for anything. Sometimes they will even take you right to a domestic violence shelter, or to someone else's home, if they cannot arrest him but you would like to leave the situation, even for a day or two.

Keep in mind that police cannot force you to get an order of protection, nor can the police or the court give him one unless you file for it. And even if you get one, you have to go through several stages of court appearances and filing paperwork for the order to come into effect or remain in effect.

*What is the point of a protective order?*

I wish I could say that a protective order provides you with 24-hour security service or armed bodyguards, but it is not that. It serves as a deterrent for an abuser to have contact with you. This theoretically allows you to move on with your life without fear that he is going to enter back into it. This is assuming that your abuser feels that leaving you alone is preferable than the risk of going to jail for not leaving you alone.

Unfortunately having a protective order is no guarantee that he is going to leave you alone. It is only a deterrent and it may be more after the fact than before the fact. If you have an order, he will go to jail if he is found guilty of breaking it. If you do not have an order, events like getting a phone call or a text or showing up at your work would not have any criminal merit under the law. The order transforms contact between you into a crime. You can use this to your advantage if you are determined to be free. It would also affect the length and type of punishment he were to receive if he committed another type of crime, such as assault upon you. The penalties will be more severe where the protective order is already in place.

*What if I just leave him without an order?*

You can try to get out without a protective order. If the relationship is early enough there might not be enough of an entanglement for him to be interested in keeping you in bondage. You might be afraid of getting the law involved and his vengeance escalating because of it, and this is reasonable. You may think that once you are broken up or divorced that you will be able to carry on conversations with your abuser, especially if it is about your children.

I warn you that if you are trying to get free, whether you have an protective order or not, your speaking to him again will only open up avenues of bondage and he will try to draw you in again with sweet words and sincere-sounding apologies and guilt trips.

Even talking about leaving can put you in a precarious situation. The most dangerous time for a woman in an abusive relationship is when you she trying to get out of it. The anger that can pour out of your abuser against your strength and determination to get out can prove dangerous or fatal. If you are afraid of him in any way, you have to weigh the advantages of having legal protection as a deterrent against him versus not aggravating a potentially violent situation by getting the law involved.

Without an order there are no legal hassles, no courtrooms, no outside intervention, and the whole matter is more private. Without an order there is also the lack of legal protection and or possible deterrent to his continued contact or harassment.

With an order you might succeed in being able to scare him away. With an order you can also aggravate him or the situation into a potentially violent or dangerous scenario. An order can deter him or it can set him off.

I did leave my abuser without an order when I bought my own home and moved away from him at the time my youngest child was a baby. My abuser continued to abuse me verbally when we had contact (which was frequent because of the children and coordinating visits and over money issues) and then I was connived into letting him move in with me, because he brainwashed me into believing he "could not support two households" and that the only way I would have any money from him was if he lived with me. It was within a few months of him living with me that he pummeled me into the floor and I called the police and I got another protective order. He left the state for over a year and sent no support to the children, who were all still very young at the time.

*Won't an order make things worse?*

Getting a protective order can make things worse. Even talking about getting an order to your abuser can make things worse, and I highly advise against ever mentioning it to him—much the same way I have advised my readers not to read Warning Signs of Abuse anywhere near their abuser. If you are planning to leave, plan to leave without ever telling him your plans and do not ever mention a protective order. If you are go to a shelter they will help you get the order, so go to the shelter first if you need to and worry about the order later.

The reality is that whether you get a protective order or not, leaving a violent or potentially violent abuser is a dangerous gamble. I know how hard it is to want to get out but have the fear of something worse happening to you or your children if you do. Nicole Brown Simpson was murdered without having a protective order and many have been able to get free and stay free with having one, such as I have managed to do so far. I highly advise counseling with the local domestic violence shelter or agency representative who can best advise your own particular situation as to whether an order is feasible in your case or not.

But as I said before, the reality is that once you have been hooked by an abuser, the potential for violence exists, even with a protective order. This is the difficult gamble of decision-making that you must weigh carefully if you are ever going to get out and stay free.

*How would you put a protective order into practice?*

Once you receive the order, it is a document that you need to keep "on your person" at all times— this can be in your car if you drive, or in your handbag. This way the police will know how to respond when you contact them or if you are out of your area. You are also supposed to deliver a copy to your local police precinct so they have a copy on file (at least that is how they do it where I live). You are supposed to call the police if he contacts you in any way. If the police feel he has violated the terms of the order, he can be arrested and charged with violating the order, in addition to any other crimes committed while violating it, such as harassment or stalking. He will try to get you to rescind the order. You may also have something to do with it.

Abusers are very crafty about finding ways to get you to see them and then get you to go back to court and rescind the abuser order. You are not supposed to see him, but somehow there are flowers left on your doorstep. Can you call that in to the police? They can make a police report, but does that prove anything? Somehow the conversation starts again— and you may even be the one to start it. It is hard to admit this, but maybe you miss him— maybe not him really, but what you were used to. You may also be used to the level of stress that the abuse brought out in you, and have become wired to situations that are stressful so you unconsciously seek them out. There may be a loneliness that sets in, which happens when you break up with anyone and don't have a new relationship right away. That loneliness can lead to a desperation that may make you call him or see him. And if you have kids there may be an excuse for either of you to have to talk on the phone.

Some protective order provisions allow for contact related to children such as discussing dropping them off for visits, but I highly recommend against any such allowances. Once you get on the phone it is easy to get beguiled by the sweet and penitent voice and the words of desire that may sneak in, from either of you. If while discussing their weekend visitation he says that he misses you and wants to have sex, are you going to report it?

A provision can be made that any arrangements relating to the children be done via a mediator. This would have to be someone willing to deal with your abuser, who may end up turning his anger and frustration at the situation to the mediator. He may also try to turn the mediator against you with accusations and stories.

The first protective order I got was even before we got married. He had punched me in my breast and he was arrested for assault. After a certain amount of time I went back and had the order rescinded. I had another many years later when we had six children already and he had socked me into the floor and I called the police. I had a welt on my face, and he disappeared from the state to avoid being arrested and I got a PFA then, too. He was eventually arrested and I eventually also had that order rescinded. There were three or four others but the counties have the records and I do not remember the details of them all. The last one was when he punched me in my breast and after he was arrested on drug charges (which he definitely could not blame on me) and it was at that point, when he was incarcerated, that I got what was to become my final PFA and began the long-overdue process of ending my relationship with him forever.

*How do you go about getting a protective order?*

In our state to get the order initially, you have to file a request at your county courthouse. One county I lived in has an organization that provides helpers to help you with the filing process, and has lawyers and legal representatives to help you when you appear before the judge.

When you first apply for an order of protection or PFA (what my state calls a "Protection From Abuse" order), you are asked various questions about what brought you there, about any specific incident of violence or abuse, and any history of violence or abuse. If you do have pictures it would be great to print them if you can or make sure they are accessible on your cellphone or computer, which you should have with you. In some cases there is a special office specifically for abuser orders or it is handled by a secretary or clerk somewhere else in the courthouse. You will have to wait for some time— if you file in the morning you may be done by lunch, or you may have to come back after lunch— but if the judge feels the order is warranted, you will be granted a "temporary order" which is good for a certain amount of time, usually ten days or so, until the abuser can be served with papers and you both have to appear in court. In some cases a judge can be called upon in the middle of the night or the weekend to sign an emergency order if the situation is deemed serious enough.

*What are the results of a protective order?*

There are some serious results of a protective order. He can be ordered to stay away from your domicile, even evicted— if you live together; he can be ordered to have no contact with you of any kind; you will be granted temporary full custody of your children; you may be eligible for certain types of emergency public assistance. If he calls you, or stalks you, or comes to your home or work, or sends you a text or email or letter, destroys your property, or worse, actually finds a way to you and physically attacks you, he will be arrested for violating the order, in addition to being arrested or charged with anything he did to you: assault, battery, terroristic threatening, stalking, harassment, rape or sexual assault, attempted murder or any combination of these, if he is caught.

And with a protective order, there are stipulations for you as well. You are under orders not to have contact with the abuser. You are not to call him, email him, text him, send selfies, send packages, send messages through other people, go on any webcams, visit his social media pages, go by where he is staying, see him, or the very worst, have sex with him. If you do any of these things he can bring you back to court to have the order dismissed. And if you wish to bring the order to a permanent status, the fact that you have been in contact will make it difficult for a judge to make a clear decision on granting the order.

Imagine the level of indignation that arises from a man who is not only kicked out of his home but denied rights to his children, and forbidden by law to talk to you. Protective orders may be helpful to some women in some situations, but some abusers will see it as a personal attack on their ego and their identity as a man, and will seek vengeance upon you for having done it. They are angry because they cannot control some part of their lives that they used to control. This can bring such rage and irrationality and this is why protective orders seem good on paper but in reality can be dangerous in some situations.

But since the mind of an abuser is narcissistic, if it serves him to leave you alone to avoid risking jail he just may do that and fold, with his tail between his legs, and look for another target or victim elsewhere. But within an abuser is the furious need to control, and control you— and when that becomes irrational or all-consuming, as it is for many abusers, they will still try to contact you, or come after you, because they think they are invincible and because their anger is greater than their logic. This is when women have acid thrown on their faces, get shot in the face, get their throats slashed, or get burned alive, or at the very least are threatened and made to fear.

*What if I call him or see him?*

I do believe that judges and the whole judicial system is wiser and more sensitive about domestic violence and abuse than perhaps in my mother's generation and in my grandmother's generation. My mother was married to an abuser who became a Satanist and terrorized my younger half-siblings— but in the court system in the 70's she was treated with contempt and sexism. During that 60's my grandmother went to the police with a slash on her face, and was told by police that the injury could have been "self-inflicted." No one arrested her abuser for that, or for trying to throw her out a fourteen-story balcony. I think the system has improved greatly since the '70s.

I think judges understand better now if you were coerced or tempted into contact after establishing an abuse order. And I myself understand how difficult it is to keep even wanting the order even after you are granted one. Maybe I was wrong to do this? What he did wasn't so bad after all. Maybe he will be different after all. I don't know if I can go through with this. This is causing more problems than solving them. Still, keeping resolve is one of the greatest challenges in getting and maintaining a protective order, as well as getting out of an abusive relationship in general.

*What happens when I get to court?*

What used to upset me was having to appear in court with my abuser in the same room. Sometimes he was only a few feet from me. It was as if I could hear his breathing and I felt he was watching me. Sometimes I would deliberately sit in the back of the courtroom so he could not sit behind me and I could avoid the feeling like he was breathing down my neck. In some cases they will separate the victim and the abuser and keep them in separate rooms or areas until called before the judge.

It would be very helpful for you to have a friend or family member or minister go with you to any protective order hearings, even if you have the additional support of domestic violence workers or legal representation. The day I got my final PFA order, the temporary order had been effect for six months, and I had not spoken to him for six solid months— the first time in twenty-four years that I had accomplished that. During the hearing phase, where we both had to go up before the judge and he was standing a few feet to the left of me. He obfuscated and hemmed and hawed at the judge during questioning and even having to listen to his voice as he stood a few feet from me was horrible. When the judge signed the order, she remarked that our was "an old case" and that these problems had been going on "for a long time." She then scolded my abuser that I was "not his property" and that he was ordered to "leave [me] alone" and that he had to understand that the reason I was getting this order was because I wanted "nothing more to do with him." I was granted the permanent order and he was ordered to pay the court costs. He was kept by an armed officer while I was permitted to leave the courtroom.

I hung on my birth mother's neck as we stood to leave and sobbed my eyes out— right in front of him. This hearing and this final PFA order was the nail in the coffin of my twenty-four-year relationship and I knew it was really and finally over. It was an emotion I never felt before and have not felt since: grief, relief, vindication, sorrow, vulnerability, open wounds, death, feeling unloved, memory, regret, bitter-sweetness, celebration— all rolled into one. I did not intend to break down and it was very uncomfortable knowing he was watching me cry, but when it happened it all came rushing out of me. In the sick mind of an abuser, he was probably happy he was able to still get a reaction out of me. It would have been much harder if my birth mother had not been there to catch my tears and hold me as I wailed. It is very difficult to be in the same room with someone who hurt you enough to be in court over it, and to go at it alone might be enough to inhibit some women from completing the process.

## WHY PROTECTIVE ORDERS DON'T ALWAYS WORK

*He can still pursue you.* Some men are so obsessed with their victim and are so defined by the need for control that the irrationality and intensity of the bondage will lead them to still come after you, sometimes with greater ferocity and vindictiveness than before you got the order. How dare she! Who does she think she is? I'll show her! Just wait until I get her in bed again! She will remember what she is missing soon enough! The order only works if he breaks it, and in some cases he will break it. If he feels he can get away with the crime of breaking the order he probably will.

*You give in (the cycle of abuse).* You are either sweet-talked back into it (when you should not have been communicating) or you get lonely or you get frightened or all of the above.

*He will use your getting it against you.* If you do go back to him, he will never let you forget the nerve you had in getting the order in the first place. It might discourage you from having a go a second time.

*You change your mind.* Things get better after a while, or you begin to feel guilty that you caused him so much trouble, or perhaps you are truly afraid that having the PFA is worse for you than better for you. No matter why, if you change your mind then it becomes harder the next time to convince a judge to grant you another PFA if you change your mind and rescind it.

*He thinks you are weak.* He is playing you to see how long you can go before you break down and give in. You will see the tactics and the cunning— trying to talk to you, coming to your place of work, trying to see you at church.

*You cannot protect yourself unless you call.* If you do not get a PFA then whatever help it might provide in your situation if unavailable to you.

*A PFA cannot stop all crimes from occurring.* The sad reality is that women are killed with PFA's and women are killed without PFA's. They are not a fail-safe deterrent for any deranged man who wants to hurt you or kill you. The goal is to make contact with you illegal so that perhaps it will appeal to his narcissism and selfish in wishing to finally relent and stay away from you. But there are no guarantees with a protective order.

*You only might be able to have him arrested after the fact.* If he violates the PFA and attacks you or hurts you, then you can only get him in trouble after the fact. But at least, if he does go to jail, he will be away from you for that period of time and you will have some reprieve.

*What if it is too late?* I am not sure that it is too late at any point but it might be ineffectual if he is hell-bent on destroying you and does not care about penalty. In the worst cases you have a murder-suicide (a situation I hear about all too much these days).

## OTHER LEGAL ISSUES: SEPARATION, DIVORCE, CUSTODY, CHILD SUPPORT, AND TAXES

When you are dealing with a protective order you will in all likelihood have other legal issues that you will have to deal with, namely, separation or divorce, custody issues, child support and even taxes. The fact that if you have children you have to deal with custody and child support issues makes the problem of getting free even more difficult. Sometimes you do not feel you have the energy or wherewithal to go to another hearing or even see your abuser in court or have to fill out another set of forms.

### Separation and divorce
In some states there is a status called "legal separation." In our state there is no such legal status, so if you do separate and move out then that is it, you cannot get a document proving that you are separated legally. For some people it may suffice to be separated and not actually go to the next step of getting divorced. This may largely be for religious reasons— many religious schools of thought see

divorce of any kind— for any reason— as a sin, even if there is abuse or drugs or any other perversity involved. This can make getting out of a marriage to an abuser difficult if the victim does not believe in her own mind that what she is doing is okay. Some religious groups might condescend to allowing a legal or other separation for reasons as I mentioned.

### Child support

My abuser used to tell me that if I ever filed for child support he was going to leave the state or the country and go off the grid and I would never get any money from him. Because I did not have the financial support of any family members this was truly a terrifying threat. I guess I felt that the bird in the hand (what little erratic amounts of money he came up with to support the kids) was worth two in the bush (not knowing if I would ever be able to support the kids on my own).

As it ultimately turned out, I did get into the child support system, once when we were separated when I got my own home and as it stands today. After a stint in jail and rehab he has made some payments into the system and he cannot now hide or run away. There was a two-year period where I got nothing from him. But we all survived it. Do not let the fear of not getting child support stop you from getting out of your abusive relationship. You can get child support even if you are still legally married but are separated. There does not even need to be an actual custody order in place, unless he was fighting really hard for the kids and you needed to go to court to establish custody. If you have a protective order you will get full custody unless at the time of the order you wish to share custody for some reason.

If you have a protective order, you can request an escort into the court and escort to your car. I had a guard who stayed in the room with me, between us, during the entire meeting. I would also advise bringing someone who cares about you along for support. Especially if you are in the early stages of getting out, it will be very hard to see him and hear his voice and listen to his bullcrap when he talks to the judge or adjudicator. This last time it was so hard for me that I had to leave the room and get fresh air because I started having an asthma attack. He was horrible and started quibbling over having to provide small amounts of money for his children. Although I had my mother with me for the final PFA hearing, I went alone to the child support hearing. That was one of the worst days in the life of my dead relationship with my abuser.

At any rate, the amount we settled on was a pittance, and as of this writing it has been modified to be even less. So what do I do? I take a deep breath and sigh, and wish I had done this years ago, because it is not as bad as I thought it was going to be. We all in this family learn to live on less than most people we know, and I for one am glad that I am not materialistic or consumer-driven or covetousness. I truly am content with what I have. I don't even enjoy buying things anymore. My girls are learning to be patient, because it takes longer than they or I would like for me to get things for them, but overall they have great strength of character and are less petty and superficial and indulged than many of their peers.

*Of what a woman is overcome, of the same is she brought into bondage*

In the end the thing that held its last thread of bondage around me was money. I was almost divorced and the man who I thought loved me for thirty years was going to marry me. But when this man devastatingly rejected me just weeks before my divorce was final, I wound up in the hospital. I came out convinced that I had no other choice than to continue to live with my abuser, the man that was then my ex-husband legally— although you probably have figured out by now that I feel I never had any "marriage" with my abuser in the first place and he never was a "husband" to me.

*Custody*
My abuser really hung this one over my head. "I will take you to court and they will take the kids away from you because you are a horrible mother and you are insane." I can tell you now that any judge would have given me custody but he scared me and made me feel like it was possible that he could do that to me. Especially when the kids were young this terrified me. You have to decide whether you need a custody arrangement or not. Some men will not agree to give child support unless they get either partial or full custody. Sometimes the arrangement becomes one of his visitation and your custody, or joint custody where you are the primary custodian. If you abuser also abused your children in any way he may be denied any custodian rights at all.

The difficulty is with the "pick up and drop off arrangement." How do you negotiate exchanging your child or children without communication that could possibly lead to trouble? In some situations an intermediary can be used, such as a relative or social worker or court-appointed guardian. You can arrange to leave the child with the intermediary at a visitation location such as park or restaurant and leave before he gets there. My point is to avoid seeing each other and communicating.

Some women are able to have minimal phone discussions with their abuser about these situations, and even some court-ordered PFA's allow for communication solely for child visitations arrangements and no more. Personally I would have a hard time with that because a neutral conversation could quickly and easily turn into an argument or a verbal altercation or an attempt at apology and reconciliation. He could get angry enough from the conversation to try something once he sees you in person later that day when you drop off your child or kids. Unless the intermediary is court-ordered he may become abusive with that person as well because of his general frustration and sense of the loss of control he has about the whole visitation reality.

I say do not speak to him directly at all. Use an intermediary, make arrangements so that you do not have to see, him or speak to him again.

*Taxes*

Things are not really so bad in this area. You can still be married and file "Head of Household." You do not have to be divorced to be separated and the head of your own household. This was a step I took for many years because I was not ready to divorce but I was providing the bulk of the support for the children. I was wise in that from the very beginning of our marriage, I never filed a joint return with him. In the earlier days I filed "Married Filing Separately" because I did not want any of his tax problems to be attached to me. You have to pay more tax overall if you file separately but you are not required to file jointly if you choose not to. Once you divorce (even with children) and if you are alone with no children you can file "Single."

Sometimes separated or divorced couples divide how they will deduct the children for tax purposes. Sometimes there is an even arrangement and sometimes it has to be battled with a lawyer or tax accountant. I highly advise consulting both if necessary to insure your returns are the most beneficial to you and your children.

My understanding is that child support is not considered income for the federal income tax and you do not and should not report child support as income. Please of course check with an accountant or the IRS for further details pertaining to your own unique situation.

One of the nice things for single mothers who are working is a refund entitled the Earned Income Tax Credit (EIC). You can get many thousands back just for working, even you are only working part-time and even if your abuser is also working. Visit the IRS website for more information on the EIC an other matters related to tax status and other issues.


STARTING OVER


Once you have gotten out you have made a big step, whether it be to your mom's house, or a hotel, or the shelter. I know it takes great bravery and resolve but you stand a good chance of an abuse-free life the sooner you heed the warning signs of abuse and make the move to get away.

But of course if he knows where the shelter is where you'll be staying or he knows your mom's address or he knows where you work, there is no telling what a very angry man could do, whether you try to get away or get a PFA or want to separate and/or divorce. No matter how simple it may be, there is always a risk that he will react badly and violently.

When I was at the shelter a gal was attacked right outside the building by her abuser because he knew where she was staying. All too often I hear of new stories of beautiful women (many with children) who are killed because they tried to leave their abuser. Sometimes the kids will die in the collateral damage of a weak, angry, and desperate boy-man. At least in some cases he kills himself as well and spares the criminal justice system the cost of his trial and incarceration.

One solution is to move very far away— but then what is your support system? You could find a network though your local domestic violence shelter; it is possible they could refer you to a shelter in another city, county or state. But the truth is that a determined abuser can find you and still stalk you and still confront you and still harm you. You need to be aware that these possibilities exist and getting away in and of itself is no guarantee you will be free from him.

Some abusers will fold their tail between their legs and retreat— possibly because they have found other prey or because they have found something else to control, or perhaps his particular appetite of control-need is not as ravenous as that of other men.

In my area there is special, long-term protective housing, which is available for clients who have stayed in the short-term shelter for a certain amount of time. You might have such an arrangement in your area.

*Get Away Planning Tips*

This may seem extreme but you could end up in an extreme situation. I highly recommend taking a self-defense class if you situation would permit it. If he has a copy of your car key you might have to change the lock if you cannot slip the key off his chain. Get a safe deposit box for things you definitely do not want him to have— your valuables, papers, even the photos taken of your injuries. Have some legal weapons on your person and in your can— pepper spray, whistle, alarm or even a gun, if you are licensed and trained and capable of using it to defend yourself and feel this is an option for you. Keep emergency supplies at a safe location that he knows nothing about, such as a friend's basement or attic.

And even if the help may not be as much as you really need, enlist the help of willing ministries, organizations churches— you may get people to help you with provisions and money and even moving, and when you find you do not have the strength yourself it helps to have help.

If you remain in your own home and he is evicted because of the PFA, do your best to secure your home. If you can, install an alarm system. Change the locks. Have your mail delivered to a P.O. box near where you work.

Again, I must say that the best-laid plans are no guarantee that you will be completely abuse-free or permanently safe from your abuser, unless he is in jail and has no one engaged to put a hit on you. This is why I hope that many women will see the warning signs of abuse well before the entanglement makes it exponentially more difficult to get out. Get out early and stay free forever!

# EPILOGUE: A FUTURE FREE FROM ABUSE

## From This Tortured Bond

From this tortured bond release me,
Do not, sovereign Lord, disdain;
For if health and freedom please thee,
Bring the antidote to pain!

For my weakened body fails me:
Always hurting, little rest;
Head and throbbing limbs ache sorely;
Twisted spinal nerves compressed;

Let alone the sacred places
Where the soul must cry alone;
Eyes and tears and voice leave traces
Wherein spirit can only moan!

Shall the dark night wane with dawning?
Do you wish me to depart?
Have you finished with me early?
Have you finished with my heart?

For time is not a friend of worth:
It ages body and soul;
Were I to join you from this earth
I'd then be fully whole.

But should you wish a warrior
To continue in this fight,

Then would you be my champion
And defend me with your might?

For I am failing in my woe,
I've not the strength to be;
One of us will have to go:
Either him, or me.

From *What Was and Is: Formal Poetry and Free Verse,*
2024.

In the summer of 2010 I obtained my divorce from my abuser. I ended up living with him after the divorce for a period of time because I couldn't afford to be on my own. After a period of time in which we did not communicate at all, a certain level of toleration on my part developed, and I was able to talk to him again. We became much like the friends we were when we first met, before the abuse began.

In 2017 he unexpectedly died from a fentanyl-laced heroin overdose. He was 57 years old.

I must say that life has been better without him in it. I have never been as happy and independent and self-sufficient as I am now, seven years after his death. I have financial means now to live on my own. My children are all grown and highly successful, and my grandchildren give me great joy.

Many of the physical symptoms I had during my time with my abuser have abated: no more fibromyalgia symptoms, no more painful fatty lumps under my skin (this is termed *adiposis dolorosa*), no more asthma, no more depression, no more bouts of insanity and craziness. I can truly say that since his death I have never been happier, more stable, and more at peace.

I have been working on my legacy— writing books and publishing and performing my poetry. My next book is to be entitled *Finally Autistic: Finding My Autism Diagnosis as a Middle-Aged Female*. I also have a new book of poetry entitled *What Was and Is: Formal Poetry and Free Verse*.

God did ultimately answer the prayer of my poem "From this tortured bond." One of us had to go, and it was him, not me.

I told my abuser, "I would rather be alone the rest of my life than continue to have to be with you." And so now I am happy and in a quieter place, and I await a future of surprises and blessings. I hope that you can experience the relief and freedom and healing that I am experiencing today, much sooner than did, and stay in it forever. I hope my life advice has been of help as you look for ways to get out early and stay free forever.

–Theresa Werba

# ADDENDUM: ABUSE SEX

*I was not sure that this chapter fit within the greater scope of the book, but it has valuable material, so I am including it here. It a most personal look at sexual abuse and is not meant as titillation or tabloid fodder. I hope the reader may find resonance in it.*

In this day and age, nothing is secret. I think back to the intrigues of the Elizabethan court scene and how so much of what really happened was hidden and obfuscated and how records were destroyed and many things that happened were never recorded at all. The value of that society was to keep secrets, rather than reveal them. And so I, too, am part of the postmodern era and not quite the anachronism that I think I am. Rather than being some kind of reality-show confession, I am sharing the following parts of my life so that if you are in an abusive relationship you can see something of what I went through in it and that you are not the only one. If you think that what you are doing with your partner or husband is good or okay, maybe what I am sharing will help change your mind. I am not attempting to write a sordid tell-all but only to share the pain that I suffered and how traumatized I became from so many years of sexual abuse. I know women have worse or weirder or more dangerous things done to them. This is my story nonetheless.

In the beginning it may have been hot and we may have been horny, but in the end he was still horny and I would close my eyes, grit my teeth, and do everything I could to make him finish quickly. We may have kissed in beginning but after the full nature of abuse was in play we did not kiss. In fact I have been told by those experienced in these things, that when a man is paying for sex he and the prostitute do not kiss.

I may have had a regular and ordinary vagina in the beginning, but after having six children he used to laugh at me in front of other people and share with them the lovely analogy that having sex with me was "like throwing a crowbar into an empty room." I ended up having not one, but two pelvic floor reconstructive surgeries to repair the uterine and bladder prolapses, vaginal stretching, and rectocele that developed from my having such large children through my petite body—two ten-pound babies, two nine-pound babies and two eight-pound babies.

Of course that wasn't the only thing that stretched and sagged after having children. I am thankful and grateful that I was able to conceive, carry, birth, nurse and raise six children, but after your breasts are full of milk for thirteen years they are not the same afterwards. When I would complain about my deflated boobs he would say, "Well, those are my boobs" and "those nipples belong to me." Then I would say to him, "Er, no, they are my nipples" and "Sorry, but my boobs belong to me." I don't remember him ever saying he was appreciative about all my body had done to bring his children into the world and raise them with the best milk and mothering and nurturing they could possibly have had. I think about having a boob job all the time, every time I see myself naked, even though I know it is vain and futile really, especially at my age.

But sometimes if I was nursing one of the babies he would slide next to me and start humping me and try to penetrate me from behind and I told him I was nursing but he didn't care. It was a one-way experience and I just focused on my beautiful baby while he was getting off. I was not charged in any way from that and his approach eventually repulsed me. In the end it was a ten-to-thirty second experience of pleasure for him and a ten-to-thirty second experience of dread for me, which I tried to speed up as quickly as I could. In the very end I used to beg him in tears to leave me alone and not come near me and not to sleep in my bed.

*Get out of my bed!*
One of the tools I tried to use to keep him out of my bed was the fact that my bed was my bed. When I moved out with the kids in 2001 I was able to purchase an expensive Tempur-Pedic mattress as a medically prescribed bed. This fortuitous event occurred because I was diagnosed with fibromyalgia—overall chronic body pain and fatigue that I have suffered with since my 30's and still suffer with today. I have had the bed for thirteen years now and it helps me a great deal with the pain and associated sleep disorder that I have, and I lay on it most of the time when I am home because I hurt so much. At the time I purchased my bed, my abuser was still functional enough to have been working fairly regularly, and his trade union provided him—and the kids, and me as his wife—with health insurance. I was able to have the bed paid for and a custom box spring made and the whole thing delivered for a few hundred dollars, because the insurance paid 80 per cent of the cost of the bed. I paid for it with my own money, and in no way did he buy the bed or give me any money for buying the bed. When I stupidly let him move in with me at my own house after we had already separated, I felt that my precious and beautiful bed had indeed been tarnished by him being in it.

"Get out of my bed!" I would tell him. "It's not your bed," he would say. "Of course it is my bed. You know it is my bed. I bought it myself." "Yeah, with my money"," he would reply. "No, I bought it with my money and the insurance paid 80 per cent." "It was my money because my insurance that helped buy it. So it is my bed." This is the kind of specious argument we would get into, because I hated him being in my bed so much and did not want him sleeping in my bed.

I used to dread it if I had to bend down to pick something up when he was around, because he would come up behind and start to ram himself on me, over and over again. "Let me put it in from behind," he would beg. I told him if he likes his penis near a butt so badly then go find some guy to do it with but to leave me alone. Countless times it was really more like male homosexual sex or animal sex and not about a male and a female human facing each other in conventional heterosexual sex. Fortunately for me, he never was able to penetrate me anally, although he had alluded to wanting to quite a bit and tried pressing against me there. But I think for him it was better if he did not see my face when he was getting off anyway, because then he did not have to face me, and confuse my frowns and winces for the joys of climax.

He used to beg me and coerce me into fellating him, even though he knew I had TMJ dysfunction and that I suffered debilitating headaches and jaw pain since I was in my early 20's. Not only did the MRIs show degeneration in the joints, but I was prescribed a mouth guard for teeth grinding and eventually had joint surgery, which has helped some since. But I used to tell him how much it would hurt my jaw if I did it, and how much it would hurt afterwards. "Well, you used to do it to [previous boyfriend], and you said he had such a big dick, so why not me?" He accused me of lying about the pain, since I was able to do it to the bigger penis from my past. He declared that I just didn't want to, as was using my TMJ as an excuse. He kept telling me that I was not really being loving to him because I would not do this for him, and that I was depriving him in some way of his rights as a husband and a man. The fact that he kept pressuring me over the years did cause me to give in sometimes. Of course, he would rub it in how I only did it a few times, and how I obviously liked the other guy's big penis more. Towards the end I figured out a way to hold in my unstable right jaw joint with my fingers during the event in order to minimize the pain I was having, get through it, and minimize the pain afterwards.

*What sex is not*
No matter how severe the level of sexual abuse you may have suffered, the fact that you have suffered abuse at all and realize it indicates that there are reasons you thinking about or trying to get out of your relationship or marriage. We are not animals, no matter what the evolutionists like to tell us, and the sexual relationship between a male and female is supposed to be better than that of animals. In most cases the male of the animal species seeks and mounts the female, and she attracts him, in order to reproduce. Their organs are complimentary for this reason. But as humans we can expect and can experience something much more than this. Sex can truly be making love—an extreme expression of one's love for one's lover or partner or spouse. It is not meant to be man's pleasure at the expense of woman's pain. It is not meant to be "gimme gimme" but a glorious give and receive.

Sex is not love, but it may sometimes feel like love. Abuse sex is definitely not love. Orgasm may feel like love, but it is not love. No doubt those three girls trapped in that house in Cleveland for over ten years were brought to orgasm by their abuser, but there is not a shred of love in what happened to them. If a man forces sex on you that is rape and not love. If he coerces you into sex it might not exactly be rape but it is not love. Making derogatory remarks about your body or body parts or your sexual performance is not love. Using religion, or guilt, or threats to get you to engage in sex is not love.

Many of you know this already. You are coming to feel, or already do feel as I came to feel, that sex with your abuser is abuse. And some of you are either forced to continue in sex with your abuser, or acquiesce to it, because you find some benefit to it. He might actually be nicer afterwards, for a little while. You may feel safer because you are on his "good side" if you give him what he wants. You are hoping maybe that if you oblige him he will change, or not get any worse. You may feel that what limited control you have over your life might just be that fact that you can choose to open your legs or your mouth. You may be deluded by the momentary rush of orgasm and the afterglow into thinking things are okay between you. You may still be horny enough that you want sex too, and are willing to look past the coercion and the insults and the fear to get it.

I know that if I were confronted by a stranger who was going to rape and kill me, I certainly would let him rape me, and I would do everything I could to make him enjoy it, if he would just let me go afterwards. I felt that way in my relationship with my abuser for so long. I just wanted to appease him, make him happy, keep him from getting angry, keep the peace, so he would not hurt me or make things worse.

The desire to be loved by my abuser and appreciated and desired for who I am was killed a long time ago. Some of you may still feel love towards your abuser, no matter how he is treating you. Some of you honestly believe or have been taught to believe that "the marriage bed is undefiled" and so that means he can do whatever he wants to you or demand or take anything he wants from you, no matter how you feel about it or whether you want it or not. Again, this hearkens back to the notion of a "submissive" wife when utilized in its most misogynistic forms.

I know there are people out there who are into dominant/submissive sexual relationships. There are women who like being dominant and who are even paid for being dominant, and men who actually like receiving pain from a woman for sexual pleasure. I find the lot of it perverse from any angle. I cannot support any relationship where one person dominates another or holds another person in bondage, whether this is sought out willingly or forced on another person. Something is clearly wrong with all of that. The ideal sexual relationship between a male and female is one of respect, and mutual vulnerability, and compassion, and tenderness and encouragement and nakedness of soul as well as body. I cannot advocate for any less for any reason. If you like fifty shades of grey I definitely prefer the warm sunlight and encourage you to go sit in the sun instead.

I just used sex as a tool and a defensive weapon. Ask yourself honestly if this is what you want and if getting out would be better than staying. Women were designed to be the object of highest love, beauty and value. At least getting away can give you a chance for something healthy and normal and beautiful and good and better than it is now. You will never know the taste of pure, fresh-squeezed juice if you settle for Kool-Aid.

I do hope that you will understand that if you are being sexually abused that you are worth more than that, and that you should consider getting out of the relationship, either via separation or breakup or divorce and possibly the use of a protective order. It will never get better and you will never be happy and you will continue to suffer psychologically and you will eventually find it difficult and ultimately impossible to function. I hope that the material in the previous chapters will give you help and impetus to get out early and stay free forever.

# ACKNOWLEDGMENTS

I wish to thank my editor Terry Heisey, who did a superlative job in "seeing what I cannot see, " and who gave me much impetus to "keep writing" and finishing this book.

I wish also to thank Carla Christopher, who has believed in what I am trying to do and has given me much encouragement and validation as a poet, a writer, a survivor of abuse, and as a woman. You indeed were the impetus for my picking up the manuscript again and finishing what I started a year and a half ago.

Thank you Graziella Sarno, attorney for Berks Women in Crisis, who told me it would take seven attempts to get free, and it did.

Thank you Demetra Dunlop, for reading every email, listening to every sobbing cry, taking those phone booth and hospital phone calls, and staying steady against so many years of turmoil. I could not have made it out without you.

Thank you Mom, for being one of the only people in my life who truly understood what I was going through, and who stayed tenacious for so many years in the conviction that I needed to get out and be free. You helped me walk through all the steps along the way and help me find validity when all around me was despair.

Thank you my beautiful children: Francesca, Angelica, Anthony, Gloria, Gabriella, and Sophia, for enduring all that you endured and still endure. You are each and all fine adults of whom I am most proud.

# SOURCES AND RESOURCES

There are a plethora of sources and resources that deal with domestic violence and abuse that you can find by a few clicks of the mouse and your search engine. There are some of the things I have found helpful during the writing of this book. It is by no means exhaustive but gives you some of the references I found helpful and some other things you might find helpful.

National Domestic Violence Hotline 800 799 7233
www.thehotline.org
This website and phone number will connect you to someone who will listen and give you local referrals if needed

*Warning Signs of Abuse* Interview with Theresa Werba (formerly Theresa Rodriguez)
https://www.bardsinger.com/warningsignsofabuse
I describe *Warnings Signs of Abuse* and how women caught in abuse can benefit from reading it

"Psychopath" (on YouTube)
Fascinating documentary with real-life psychopaths talking about their psychopathy

*The Mask of Sanity* by Hervey Cleckley
https://cassiopaea.org/cass/sanity_1.PdF
An interesting book which describes the psychopathic personality. Free download

The Nicole Brown Simpson Foundation
www.nicolebrownsimpson.blog
The website for the foundation in honor of Nicole Brown Simpson, founded by her sister Denise

*Nicole Brown Simpson: The Private Diary of A Life Interrupted* by Faye Resnick. Beverly Hills: Dove Books, 1994. One of Nicole's best friends tells the story of her life and death at the hands of OJ Simpson

*Without A Doubt* by Marcia Clark. New York: Viking Books 1997. The story of the OJ trial from the point of view of the lead prosecutor    In Contempt by Chris Darden. New York: Viking Books 1996. The story of the OJ trial from the point of view of one of the lead prosecutors

*Diagnostic and Treatment Guidelines on Domestic Violence* by Elaine Carmen, MD., et al.
https://www.nlm.nih.gov/exhibition/confrontingviolence/materials/OB11102.pdf
A look at abuse from the perspective of the medical profession

*Reclaiming Our Voices: an anthology for survivors of domestic violence or sexual assault* edited by Carla Christopher-Waid, et. al., Community Arts, Inc. 2015.
https://www.amazon.com/Reclaiming-Our-Voices-Anthology-Honoring-ebook/dp/B00VO8Y8RS
Hear the voices of other who have survived different forms of abuse (I have a truncated excerpt from Warning Signs of Abuse in it)

# ABOUT THE AUTHOR

Theresa Werba the author of seven books, four in poetry: *Jesus and Eros: Sonnets, Poems and Songs* (Bardsinger Books 2015), *Longer Thoughts* (Shanti Arts 2020), *Sonnets* (Shanti Arts 2020) and *What Was and Is: Formal Poetry and Free Verse* (Bardsinger Books 2024). Her work has appeared in such journals as *The Scarlet Leaf Review, The Wilderness House Literary Review, Spindrift, Mezzo Cammin, The Wombwell Rainbow, Fevers of the Mind, The Art of Autism, Serotonin, The Road Not Taken,* and *the Society of Classical Poets Journal.* Werba holds a Bachelor of Arts in vocal music performance from Skidmore College and a Master of Music with distinction in voice pedagogy and performance from Westminster Choir College. Werba is a member of the National Association of Teachers of Singing and has been a contributing writer for Classical Singer Magazine, where she has written on a myriad of topics of interest to classical singers. Her recording *Lullabies: Traditional American and International Songs* may be found on streaming services. Werba is the joyful mother of six children and grandmother to seven. Find Theresa Werba at www.bardsinger.com and on social media @thesonnetqueen.

* 9 7 8 0 9 6 5 6 9 5 5 1 0 *